AT
THE PLEASURE
OF THE BOARD

AT
THE PLEASURE
OF THE BOARD

The Service of the
College and University President

By Joseph F. Kauffman

AMERICAN
COUNCIL ON
EDUCATION One Dupont Circle • Washington, D.C. 20036

© 1980 by American Council on Education
One Dupont Circle, Washington, D.C. 20036

Library of Congress Cataloging in Publication Data
Kauffman, Joseph F
At the pleasure of the board.

1. College presidents. I. Title.
LB2341.K36   378′ .111   80-10418
ISBN 0-8268-1440-9

9 8 7 6 5 4 3 2 1
Printed in the United States of America

To Rose Davidson

Contents

Foreword

$\mathbf{M}$y attention was first drawn to Joseph Kauffman when he was dean of students at the University of Wisconsin (now Wisconsin—Madison) in the 1960s. As dean of students, he was one of the rare student-watchers of the period who were neither starry-eyed about the "idealistic" young people who were so "heroic" and so much "wiser" than their stuffy elders in pushing for change. Nor did he lose his empathy (quite a different quality from sympathy) for the real problems these young people faced.

The governance reforms which students helped put in place in the late 1960s and early 1970s have caused many of the problems encountered today by college and university presidents and in the presidential search process described in this book. Those reforms democratized the search process and forced in many states the passage of so-called sunshine laws. The laws made selection public, thus eliminating from consideration, as Kauffman notes, many persons who did not want to expose their interest in the job lest the position already held would be weakened by such a sign of disaffection. The laws also led to procedures in which selection committees became more politicized, and members had to act in the presence of the press and those spokespersons for various constituencies who would turn candidates' visits into inquisitions.

The college and university presidency is an anomalous role, for no career line serves as preparation for it. Nor does the position carry security; the president serves "at the pleasure of the board"—the average length of service is five years. Unless he or she is young enough to change careers (go back to teaching in many cases) or famous enough to land one of the few foundation or consultant positions available, security is, at best, uncertain. Outside the State University of New York (SUNY) system, there is no assurance of a postpresidential position. In consequence of such insecurity, many college and university presidents may be serving at the displeasure of the boards but, because of board inertia, are perhaps hanging on, feeling trapped in their positions, and would leave if they could find any suitable place to go. As Kauffman points out,

Foreword

the relatively modest salaries presidents are paid (in public institutions, salaries are often tied to how much a governor or a system president makes) are no recompense for the incumbent's loneliness and frustration and for the fishbowl existence of the family.

Although there is no preparation for the job or full recognition of its hazards, some efforts are made at on-the-job training, for example, the educational leadership institutes offered by the American Council on Education for new college and university presidents. These week-long sessions often lead to the important discovery that one's private miseries are shared by others—not a cure for loneliness, but some solace. The agenda may concentrate on issues relevant in the public sector, such as collective bargaining procedures, but may be quite beside the point for the presidents of small church-related colleges, only a handful of which have as yet experienced unionizing campaigns. Various workshops are run for both presidents and prospective academic leaders, such as the Institutes for Educational Management at the Harvard Graduate School of Education. The State University of New York holds summer retreats at Rensselaerville for SUNY chief executive officers, where they can share problems in an unusually frank atmosphere.

The healing sharing of experience described forms an important part of *At the Pleasure of the Board*. For example, readers will appreciate Dr. Kauffman's drawing on his exposure to a unionized campus when he served from 1968 until 1973 as president of Rhode Island College. After leaving Rhode Island College to become professor of higher education at Wisconsin, he decided to interview presidents of both private and public institutions as a basis for preparing this book.

The thirty-two presidents Kauffman interviewed (a third of whom had left their positions by two years later) agreed about the importance of leadership to counteract the present malaise in academic institutions. Despite their commitment, most were burnt out after a short period, consumed by the unrealism of the faculty (and activist students) about institutional survival, let alone distinction; the relative irresponsibility of boards, which until recently enjoyed the honorific status without being able or willing to do the work necessary to help presidents; and the lack of understanding by the public, faculty members, and students of how limited is the president's actual power.

This power is different from the expectations that most boards entertain during a search. In his examination of the presidential selection process, Kauffman illustrates a common flaw: the use of unweighted, unevaluated criteria to select presidents. Boards (or in system states, the system head) have not thought through what major qualities are required for their institutions. They have asked for *all* the qualifications that would embody in one person the dynamism of William Rainey Harper of Chicago, the egalitarian or populist ethos of Andrew Dickson White of Cornell, the scholarly qualities found in the presidents of some top-flight liberal arts colleges and, occasionally, research universities, the public relations skills of a politician, and the charisma of an evangelist raising funds to build a television church. Having been involved in search procedures over the years, I think the unrealistic expectations sketched by Dr. Kauffman are in no way overdrawn. In choosing a president who appears to please the various constituencies, which are now drawn into the democratized and frequently overpublicized search, the regents or trustees are really ducking the issue of what missions they believe their institution should emphasize. Instead, they seek all potential missions, which is a sure road to dilution of quality in the public sector and to probable unviability in the private sector.

Presidents' frustrations in trying to serve diverse interests, as Kauffman shows, are at their worst for those who are the campus presidents in state systems. Indeed, a great virtue of this book is its treatment of the growing number of states that have put all their public institutions of higher education under a single system. Among the consequences for presidents and chancellors in the systemwide operation is the reduced "middle management" scope for action by the campus executive. For example, where there is a system chancellor and chancellor's staff, the faculty often make direct appeals, bypassing the proper procedure through their own campus executive and staff. Especially in systems, the growth of unionism, the resistance of tenured faculty to adapt to change, and the decline of collegiality, all have eroded the presidential position.

One effect of a system on a campus has been the loss of the "private spaces" about which Berkeley's Martin Trow has written—one of the wisest commentators on American higher education. These private spaces are the little nooks and crannies where students and faculty may gather for coffee or simply to chat. Trow notes how systemwide controls, which assign space as well as staff by formula, get rid of what is often most valuable in the interstices of a curriculum. The growth of unionism, in his view, is both a product and producer of a deprofessionalization of faculty members who feel that they have no real say over the actual conditions of their work, including such matters as space as well as the more bargainable issues of wages and hours. If faculty members are to be treated as employees, they conclude they might as well have the power they believe to be associated with employee unions. (In my observation, these academic unions often behave like the railroad unions in resisting changes that actually would save jobs in the long run but demand of some members inconvenience in the short run in shifting their specialties and clienteles.)

The fate of presidents in office and presidents "released" is something boards seem especially to neglect. A number of states have adopted the SUNY system of periodic presidential appraisal, but without SUNY's policy of providing every president with tenure somewhere in the system. The result may well be that the president is, in a sense, constantly up for election or that the time for reappraisal is at hand just when tough political decisions are to be made—something not unfamiliar in our political leadership. The conclusion I draw from the book is that potential presidents should have go-betweens to arrange with boards for severance pay or other protections if the "pleasure of the board" should change. (The go-between could be a lawyer, though litigation has been one of the curses that give presidents the sense of being besieged.) Such agreements would serve the institutions as well. Presidents are sometimes retained in sympathy for their dilemma in finding other employment. Such agreements would serve both institution and president when a president's initial pleasure at the chance to become an educational leader is frustrated by the inescapable ceremonial tasks, the endless grievance procedures and lawsuits, and the other frustrations characteristic of leadership in America generally when cynicism and distrust have become so widespread.

Kauffman believes that, despite the possibility of excesses, an open search procedure is essential to legitimate a president. He would like, as I would, installation ceremonies further to legitimate the office. But the legitimation is short-lived, and the first decision that adversely affects a noisy constituency can bring it to an end. No wonder presidents are lonely.

Dr. Kauffman brings to this volume the breadth of his personal experience as an executive officer, as participant in search committees, and as a long-time student of the subject. The contributions from the wide-ranging interviews with presidents illuminate the author's observations. In the large literature on the college presidency, to my knowledge, the concrete evidence and detail make *At the Pleasure of the Board* unique. This book should be of great assistance to boards of trustees in selecting presidents, to candidates who are going through that process, and to presidents in office.

DAVID RIESMAN

Cambridge, Massachusetts

Preface

This work grows out of more than three decades of work in higher education and a concern with human development. My interest in the college presidency, however, grew out of my actually *experiencing* that role when I was president of Rhode Island College (1968–73). Understanding, intellectually, what a president does is far different from being a president.

Following my return to a professorship, I made the study of leadership and the academic presidency my principal research interest. My first work was on the process of selecting college presidents. This endeavor was followed by studies of the problems of new college and university presidents and presidential evaluation or assessment. *At the Pleasure of the Board* puts all my thoughts on the college and university presidency in one essay.

This volume, then, contains both research data from my various studies and material from my experiences as a president and a consultant. Further, it expresses my growing concern over what is happening to college and university presidents. Because of this concern, *At the Pleasure of the Board* is a personal statement rather than a dispassionate review of data. My compassion for presidents and my empathy for the trials of the presidential role will be self-evident.

Since, at my stage in life, one can never be sure what will be written in the future, I would like to acknowledge the generous assistance I have received from others in gaining my knowledge and experience. First, I wish to thank the Ford Foundation and Fred E. Crossland, especially, for the support they have given me in my work on the presidency. I have also had many mentors, and I want to name Abram L. Sachar, Lawrence E. Dennis, Robben W. Fleming, Martha Peterson, Fred H. Harrington, and H. Edwin Young in that category. Many other people have been important to me in my work: Logan Wilson, Roger Heyns, Harold Enarson among them. A special note is necessary for David Riesman, an intellectual hero of mine whose friendship these past few years is enormously appreciated.

There are many others, far too numerous to mention here, who have assisted me. Special appreciation goes to Marcy Massengale for her editorial assistance and to Cleo Coenen for her stenographic aid which was so crucial in preparing the manuscript.

I have included the observations of many of the "subjects"—the new presidents—in this book, without citation, particularly in chapters four, eight, and nine. I have reported portions of the interviews previously in "The New College President: Expectations and Realities," *Educational Record*, Spring 1977, pp. 146–68, and in "The College President: Expectations, Realities, Myths," presented at the seventeenth Annual Meeting of the American Association of State Colleges and Universities, Washington, D.C., 1978.

Of course, final responsibility for the contents of this volume must be borne solely by me. As do other former college presidents, I know that credit is to be shared widely, but that the responsibility is mine alone.

JOSEPH F. KAUFFMAN

Madison, Wisconsin

1/ Introduction

**The President shall be elected by the Board of Regents,
be responsible to it, and
*serve at the pleasure of the Board.***

I have pondered, from time to time, the quaint language found in almost all governing board bylaws and repeated in all letters of appointment received by new college and university presidents. "The President shall serve at the pleasure of the Board." It makes sense, of course, for the lay board of citizens who are legally responsible for an institution to retain an executive officer in their employ and, as their agent, only as long as they wish. The board, as a corporate body, must have confidence that their agent is carrying out policies in a manner intended by the board.

The president, as chief executive officer of an institution, is really the only employee directly hired or fired by the governing board. All others come to the attention of the board upon the recommendation of the president or other administrative officers. These teaching and administrative staff usually have some form of contractual or other security which diminishes the opportunity for arbitrary or capricious actions against them. Only the president "serves at the pleasure of the board."

A rush of questions come to mind. Just what is the "board's pleasure"? How does one please or displease a board? Is not this status ambiguous for a chief executive, too vague to tolerate? How does it come to be that at the height of one's career effectiveness, one is placed in such a vulnerable situation? Most people work toward increasing job security. Why not a college president?

This volume deals with the subject of the service of the college and university president. The concept of "service" is an important legacy of the presidency, and it accompanies the corollary concept of serving only so long as it "pleases" the board. In the rich and complex history of colleges and universities, at least in the North American, English, and continental traditions, leadership was a temporary role, rotated by election among fellow scholars. The role is no less political today, and it is increasingly temporary. Certainly, anyone who fills that role knows that the service is often unappreciated.

We must restore the concept of service to the role of the presidency.

The incentives of honor, security, or material gain are simply not there any longer, if they ever existed. Good men and women of vision and courage must assume such roles, no matter how temporary they become. Only the concept of service can be an appropriate incentive. We must restore a proper respect for service in an enterprise often disparaged as an industry, utility, or supermarket.

In this book, I attempt to describe the presidency, with some perspective on the past in order to understand the present and imagine the future. My term as a college president and, especially, my interviews with presidents have given me new understanding that I wish to share with readers.

Among the topics considered are the various methods of selecting college and university presidents. I have written extensively on this (1974). My experience since then leads me to additional thoughts and criticism of the process, which I want to share, along with some recent examples of the selection process.

Additional subjects discussed include the special problems experienced by new presidents, the relationship of governing board to the president, the challenge of the growing centralization of administration and the problems of leadership in multicampus systems of colleges and universities. The advent of collective bargaining as a version of governance is also examined, with special emphasis upon its effect on the presidency. In addition, the personal side of the presidency is examined.

The volume concludes with my own experience and views on the subject of presidential evaluation and a look at the kinds of leadership we require in higher education in the 1980s—variously described as the decade of the steady-state or decline. It seems clear that it will be a turbulent decade for higher education.

In this volume, I use the term "president" generically, although "chancellor" would carry the same meaning in some systems of multicampus universities. It is only in chapter six, where I deal with such systems, that I attempt to differentiate a system executive officer from a campus or institution head.

Similarly, "governing board" refers to both institutional and system governing boards, whether they are called trustees, regents, governors, curators, or other titles.

The college and university presidency is a crucial role that is more important than ever before. It may be true that we have moved from a description of the presidency that implied total domination of an institution to a contemporary description of the presidency that implies an impermanence. Nevertheless, such changes in conception or reality do not deny the importance of the president. He or she occupies the key position in the institution; the link between the internal and external constituencies; the person who voices the values and purposes for which the institution stands. It is the president who must articulate the *potential for service* of our institutions of higher learning.

Finally, in this volume I have tried to impart to the reader something about the reality of the presidential experience. I sometimes refer to it as the phenomenology of the presidency—how the presidency is experienced by the men and women who occupy such positions. Most of what we think we know about the problems of leaders comes from people who are not leaders themselves. Perhaps the novelists and poets can portray the truth better than anyone else, yet my experience and knowledge of college and university presidents lead me to make this attempt. Above all, I wish the readers to develop the empathy and compassion that I believe our presidents deserve.

In 1904, William Rainey Harper, the first president of the University of Chicago, expressed a similar concern for the college president:

> The college president deserves the support of the intelligent man of modern times. His position is a trying one; his burden is heavy, and the reward is, at best, meager. His effort is always intended to serve the interests that make for truth and the higher life. He is not usually a "liar" or a "boss." He may sometimes seem to be too self-satisfied; one could name a few such. But for the most part he does his work, conscious that he has the shortcomings which mark his kind, realizing keenly that his tenure of office, unlike that of his colleagues, is quite uncertain, yet fully resolved to perform his duty without fear or favor and to allow time to determine the question of his success or failure (p. 186).

2/ The College Presidency—Yesterday and Today

O ne difficulty in trying to discuss the college or university presidency is the widely varying conceptions of the role portrayed in different times and places. There are so many images from the past, so many conflicting and contradictory ideas of what a president does, or ought to do. Each person brings an image, a memory, an expectation to this subject. Some historical perspective on the role of president perhaps will clear the mists and show how recurrent are the themes and fashions we often believe to be unique to our own times.

David Henry, in his report *Challenges Past, Challenges Present*, provided us with a picture of the trauma experienced by colleges and universities during the Great Depression of the 1930s. He portrayed the demands for retrenchment, the faculty anger at administrators, the cries for accountability and external controls, the scapegoat treatment higher education received, and the loss of confidence in the social significance of higher education. It has a familiar ring for our experiences today.

A review of the published writing on the college presidency of the past reveals familiar themes and concerns. Considering the relatively small number of individuals involved, there is a considerable amount of literature on and about the presidency. An annotated bibliography issued by the U.S. Office of Education (1961) describes 700 publications from 1900 to 1960 solely on the subject of the college president. The annotations give one a broad sense of what was written in the first half of this century about this unique role and person. The titles of articles include familiar subjects, from "The Vacant Presidencies" (1920) to "What Professors Want in a President" (1959); from "Women as College Presidents" (1902) to "The Burden of the College Presidency" (1905). The annotation for the latter includes: "The average man does not realize how much we demand of our college presidents."

The earliest colleges in America were founded by Protestant religious denominations; and their presidents were ministers. Unlike the governance of the medieval universities of Europe, these colleges reflected the new concept of lay participation in governance by boards of trustees. That Protestant concept still prevails, in the public and independent sectors. Thus, the beginnings of higher education in the United States cannot be understood without an appreciation for our lay boards of control and the establishment of a uniquely American office of the president.

The "old-time" college president calls forth a variety of images. Henry Dunster, president of Harvard College, was the first American academic president. Usually the president was the only semipermanent member of the college staff, for the faculty was often made up of young future clerics supporting themselves through the tutoring of young boys. Thus, the early president taught, especially the courses in ethics and moral philosophy; as a minister, he preached to his students in chapel; and he promoted his college by establishing effective relations with denominational leaders, patrons, and parents. In many ways, the early college president *was* the college. Its identity became a reflection of his character, leadership, and personal success. One image we still retain in our memory today, especially in the small liberal arts college, is that of the college as the "lengthened shadow" of its president. It is an image that still carries a burden of expectation.

Evolution of Institutional Missions and Presidential Roles
The latter half of the nineteenth century saw the development of colleges in the West, the land-grant college, and the university, modeled on the German concept of research and detached, scientific study. At the turn of the century, businessmen became involved in higher education as never before. Builders of great fortunes lent their names and fortunes to the creation of universities and hired strong presidents to develop their institutions. The clergyman president gave way to a more secular, sympathetic-to-science model, and a new generation of "builders." The names of successful businessmen such as Rockefeller, Clark, Johns Hopkins, Cornell, and Stanford became linked with university "builder" presidents Harper, Hall, Gilman, White, and Jordan.

Writing in 1899, the Reverend Mr. Stimson hailed the new type of president and the builders of our newest institutions.

> It is true that the typical college president, notably at the West, had long been more than a pious scholar. The men who built the Western colleges were such notable administrators that we can now look back upon their labors as akin to the original work of creation—they had to make all things out of nothing. . . . When the great epic of the Golden Age of the West comes to be written these are the men whose story will rival of the tale of the masterful Agamemnon and the far-seeing and much enduring Ulysses (pp. 451–52).

At the start of the twentieth century, the debates about the purpose of higher education took on a tone as harsh as any one hears today regarding the debasing of the liberal arts. Alarms were sounded by some observers, decrying the intrusion of business values, love of power, and the growth of bureaucratic administration in colleges and universities. In the late 1950s, we heard much of presidents having an "edifice complex" in their zeal to build more facilities and make campuses larger. The edifice complex occurred earlier at some institutions. In 1909 a Harvard faculty member wrote, "The men who control Harvard today are very little else than businessmen, running a large department store which dispenses education to the million. Their endeavor is to make it the *largest* establishment of the kind in America" (Veysey, p. 346).

Today, most presidents are having to learn the ways of the computer and to find the resources to budget their increasing use in colleges and universities. Try to imagine the conduct of administration without the telephone or typewriter! With a little imagination one can picture the effect these two inventions had in revolutionizing administration. Presidents, aided by deans, registrars, public relations staff, and secretaries, established offices separate from the faculty with functions separate from teaching and scholarship. The first book entirely devoted to college administration (C. F. Thwing) was published in 1900.

The "empire-builder" presidents and the development of a staff separate from the faculty called "the administration" were hotly criticized. Persons hostile to business values decried the naked ambition and aggrandizement that rapid growth portrayed. Perhaps the most famous critic who added to the various images was Thorstein Veblen who railed against the competitive search for prestige and dollars. His description of the university president as a "merchandiser" of good will, as a "Captain of Erudition," linked with the captains of industry and of finance, was a caricature that pleased many critics.

Shortly thereafter, Upton Sinclair in his book on American education, entitled *The Goose-Step* (p. 384), described the modern university president as "the most universal faker and the most variegated prevaricator that has yet appeared in the civilized world."

Presidents of the vigorous new or renascent universities were often criticized for their autocratic methods and for their departure from teaching and scholarly duties. Faculty members before World War I for the most part had not established the present traditions of shared governance. They complained frequently of their lack of power and of standing in the shadow of the president.

Veysey tells of Leland Stanford's selection of David Starr Jordan as the first president of Stanford, founded as a memorial to Stanford's son. Stanford selected Jordan to be president because he admired firm-minded executive ability and wanted someone who could manage things "like the president of a railroad" (p. 398).

Although it may not provide any solace to hard-pressed presidents today, faculty antagonism is hardly a new phenomenon to be associated with retrenchment or inflation. Again, a look to the past provides some perspective.

Professor James McKeen Cattell, whose father had been president of Lafayette College from 1863–83, was one of the foremost critics of "presidential autocracy." As a professor of psychology at Columbia University, he led a campaign early in the twentieth century to change the governance of universities by weakening the role of trustees and severely diminishing the authority of presidents. Writing in 1912, he called for the curtailment of the "autocratic powers of presidents," limiting their tenure of office to terms not to exceed four or five years, and paying them salaries comparable to professors. He also opposed the provision of residences for presidents. Cattell's antagonism toward presidents was unusually harsh. "In the academic jungle," he wrote, "the president is my black beast." He also recalled how he had "incited one of my children to call her rag doll Mr. President, on the esoteric ground that he would lie in any position in which he was placed" (p. 31).

Some Columbia University faculty members who agreed with Cattell helped to establish the New School for Social Research in New York City. It began *without* a president, leaving such duties to a committee of professors. That innovation was short-lived. Whatever else we may think about presidents, they do seem to be necessary.

Post–World War II Expansion
An examination of the publications about college and university presidents reveals how differing and contradictory were the role expectations. Successful alumni may have remembered fondly the personal attention of grand old "prexy" and have decried the new president's launching of a major expansion drive that was sure to change one's *alma mater* for the worse. Others may have criticized the "old-fashioned" president for continuing in the ways of the past while new-style leadership was expanding and altering the image of competitor colleges. The metaphors for presidential style were numerous and not all complimentary. One can say "fund raiser" with admiration or pejoratively. One person's "leader-visionary" is another person's "autocrat-wildman."

From pious scholar to autocrat to hero-builder, we see that the role and concept of the presidency were changing. For the most part, professors were critical of all leadership styles and the exercising of any presidential authority. As Hutchins observed (1956), the faculty really prefer "anarchy to any form of government." Yet Hutchins himself believed in the absolute necessity of strong presidential leadership.

It has been my own observation that intellectuals, especially scholars,

generally find distasteful the hurly-burly of the world of practical affairs—
the "market-place," with fund raising, budgets, the "selling" of an
endowment or a building to a businessman, and the like. Those whose
role expectation of the president is that of "scholar among scholars"
decry the public relations efforts and executive function assumed by
modern presidents. One illustration of this attitude occurred in the period
after World War II, when colleges entered a phase of intense competition
and unparalleled opportunity for growth. Some chose to take advantage
of the new era of expansion while others chose to hold on to their prewar
size, mission, and ethos. In the summer of 1949, *The American Scholar*
bemoaned the change of style in presidential leadership with its first full-
length editorial on the subject, "In Memoriam—The College President."
I cannot do full justice to it by my selection of excerpts, and I commend
the full text to all for study. After deploring the change of presidential role
from scholar-leader to public relations-fundraiser, the editorial goes on
as follows.

> This imposes on the College President the same requirements as on the
> movie star. He must seem "striking" without being original,
> "important" but not aloof, hard-working yet at the beck and call of his
> public. The college president becomes a largely factitious person who
> leads a newspaper life. . . . Meantime his connection with his college or
> university decreases from minimal to nominal. He comes back to the
> Campus to pant—or to settle a dispute with the union of janitors, or else
> to find out what *is* being taught in Economics so that he may rebut
> alumni complaints of Red propaganda. . . .
>   What the consequence will be for education considered as a collective
> art, no one can say with assurance. At the moment education is no longer
> led. It is guilelessly drifting, at the mercy of every external current, and
> with only an occasional hand at the helm. What human mind could
> possibly conceive and put into practice any clear view of education while
> at the same time acting out the all-things-to-all-men enumerated in the
> bond? The vision and diplomatic skill that are needed on the spot to
> achieve even a small part of any comprehensive program cannot be
> supplied by a president who does not live with, observe, and steadily
> influence his faculty.

It was evident in the 1950s that there was considerable conflict over
the issue of presidential leadership in higher education. Was the president
the facilitator, the caretaker, or the leader? President Emeritus Harold
W. Dodds of Princeton University wrote a book with the title *Academic
President—Educator or Caretaker?* W. H. Cowley, at the inauguration
of Roy E. Lieuallen at Oregon College of Education in 1956, declared in
his address,

> Name a great American college or university, and I'll name a commanding
> leader or leaders who held its presidency. On the other hand, name an
> institution with a brilliant but now-withered past, and I can probably

identify a weak president or faculty cabal, or the trustee clique that
stopped its progress. . . . The fact seems to be that the great colleges and
universities of this country became great under brilliant presidential
leaders and that other institutions with comparable and sometimes better
potential lagged or languished because of lack of a strong president.

Although much of the writing about the presidency in the 1950s concerned the private or independent institutions, for they perhaps com-
manded more attention than their public counterparts, the presidents
of public institutions faced similar controversy over their roles. The
accelerating enrollments called for increased appropriations, new capital
budgets with bonding and borrowing approvals, and the development of
satellite or branch campuses. Often, such requests meant an increase in
the public's taxes and the controversy over such measures affected presidents. Sometimes, too, it meant seeking new revenue sources to fund
increased support for public higher education. In New Hampshire, for
example, public support for education became tied to the revenues gen-
erated by state liquor stores, tobacco taxes, and a state lottery. This
linkage prompted at least one former president of the University of New
Hampshire to engage in a tongue-in-cheek entreaty to friends and alumni
of that university to "smoke more, gamble more, and drink more."

One of the best books ever written on the college presidency was by
Harold W. Stoke, a former president of Queens College, New York City.
Published in 1959, in the supposedly "quiet fifties," *The American College
President* ponders why a man would want to be a college president, given
the position's precarious nature and insecurity. One is not so sure Stoke
is complaining when he says of the president:

> In the eyes of the public he is responsible for everything about the place,
> good or bad. The institution is *his*—the faculty, the grounds and
> buildings, the football team—and he is held responsible for it. On the
> campus, *his* is the responsibility for the food in the dining halls, for the
> level of salaries, for the elegance of commencement occasions. The
> spotlight of publicity plays upon him so continuously that it leaves him
> not even intermittent shadows within which he and his family may make
> an unmarked move (p. 10).

Yet Stoke recognized his own ambivalence about the position. In
speculating on why a man would want to be a college president he
acknowledges the complexity of human motives, the desire to serve, and
probably the most important factor, "the restlessness of men which arises
from the sense of unused powers and energies." Then, joking about man's
impulses to adventure and danger, he repeats the reference that "being
a college president was like a small boy walking a high picket fence—
thrilled, but in constant danger of being impaled."

Stoke closes his remarks on the presidency with this observation, which I have always regarded as most insightful of the paradoxes in the college presidency:

> Those who enjoy it are not very successful, and those who are successful are not very happy. The explanation is hidden somewhere in the philosophy of power. Those who enjoy exercising power shouldn't have it, and those who should exercise it are not likely to enjoy it. One thing is clear: colleges must have presidents and it makes a great difference who they are (p. 20).

Changes in Presidential Roles in the 1960s

The 1960s began with much optimism in higher education. Higher education was a "growth industry," and it was rare to hear a negative word about its potency. Higher education was "where the action was," and knowledge was a resource eagerly sought by students, government, and industry. Colleges and universities were credited with meeting the "tidal wave" of students seeking admission and had a "can do" posture about quadrupling enrollments in the 1960–70 decade. Community colleges, for example, were founded on an average of one a week in that decade.

The early 1960s also saw a shortage of qualified faculty, and those who were outstanding were much sought after by government research funding agencies as well as other institutions. It was a time of the "academic revolution," in which faculty power asserted itself in perhaps its most arrogant period of American history.

In their book, *The Academic Revolution*, Jencks and Riesman devote the first chapter to developing their perspective on the transfer of power to the faculty. They state that most university presidents see their primary responsibility as "making the world safe for academicians" and assembling the most competent scholars that can be found. Despite the knowledge that faculty use the administration as scapegoat, Jencks and Riesman concluded that "administrators are today more concerned with keeping their faculty happy than placating any other single group" (p. 18).

It was in this context of the early 1960s that Clark Kerr contributed his idea of a multiversity. In his 1963 Godkind Lectures at Harvard University, Kerr, then president of the University of California, brilliantly analyzed the forces in our history that brought about what he termed the multiversity. With all of its diversity and inconsistency, the multiversity, said Kerr, "has no bard to sing its praises, no prophet to proclaim its vision, no guardian to protect its sanctity. It has its critics, its detractors, its transgressors. It also has its barkers, selling its wares to all who will listen—and many do." Kerr was not advocating the idea or vision of a multiversity; he was describing its reality in the 1960s.

As for the multiversity president, what should that person's role be? What was an appropriate description? Kerr provides a brief and marvelous recapitulation of all role expectations that have ever existed for American college presidents. It is perhaps the most often quoted section of this volume of lectures. It begins with "expected to be a friend of the students, a colleague of the faculty, a good fellow with the alumni," and on and on through the countless contradictions and absurdities we have held up as necessary for the effective president. After considering all the possible contradictory choices ever offered—leader-officeholder, educator-caretaker, creator-inheritor, pump-bottleneck—Kerr concludes that the president of the multiversity is all of these. But he is mostly a *mediator*. Kerr defined the first task of the mediator as establishing and maintaining "peace" among all the constituencies and their competing claims on the multiversity.

In a postscript to a 1972 edition of his Godkind Lectures, Kerr expressed the wish that he had not used "mediator" to describe a role of the president because that created so much misunderstanding. He was genuinely startled by the public reaction to the ascription. To many persons "mediator" meant "unprincipled compromise," he stated. However, leadership of a complex organization requires mediation among the diverse elements. But, Kerr concludes:

> I wish I had used a different word with different public connotations: political leader, or community leader, or campus statesman, or unifier or peacekeeper, or chief persuader, or crisis manager or agent of integration—anything but mediator (p. 143).

The most recent book (1974) describing the presidency was published under the auspices of the Carnegie Commission on Higher Education. Under the title *Leadership and Ambiguity*, Michael D. Cohen and James G. March presented what they termed an "essay on the American college presidency." Combining empirical data with speculation and the authors' own favorite organizational model ("organized anarchy"), the volume was provocative and controversial. I was one of the forty-two college presidents selected to be in their national sample, and I found their treatment of the college presidency rather patronizing. Yet those of us who "served in the trenches" cannot perhaps accept "outsiders" trying to understand what it's really like.

Cohen and March examined what they term the "normative images" of what the presidency should be and concluded that "there was no clear set of attributes that will assure success. Neither is there a well-defined model of the presidential job" (p. 57). In the field study they explored descriptive images of the presidency through the use of a role-similarity judgment exercise carried out with presidents and senior staff in the forty-two colleges in the sample. The role of president is compared and contrasted, in a variety of ways, with the roles of others: bookkeeper, business executive, foreman, labor-management mediator, mayor, clergyman, and military commander.

New Metaphors for the Presidency

The two roles seen as most similar to that of college president were, first, mayor and, second, business executive.

J. Victor Baldridge has developed the concept of a political model of university governance; the role image of mayor fits rather well the description of the political model.

One can get rather playful here in developing various metaphors for the university and then describing the appropriate presidential role or leadership image that flows from such a metaphor. Thus, if the university is seen as an enterprise existing in a competitive market, requiring eager consumers to partake of its wares, the college president becomes a super entrepreneur. If the metaphor of the symphony orchestra is used, and it often is, the presidential role is that of conductor. (One supposes that the deans occupy the first chairs of the various sections.)

In an interesting 1967 article in *Educational Record*, Charles H. Monson, Jr., develops three additional metaphors. The first of these builds on the service orientation of universities; the university is "dispensing machine" and the president is the operator. "He must keep his machine well stocked with interesting and useful products, recruit able young helpers, open new windows as new interests develop, and occasionally close out those products that don't sell" (p. 25).

A second metaphor is the university "zoo." Here the interesting professors are the exhibits, and the president is the keeper. Professors perform, and students are the spectators. The president must keep his exhibits lively and interesting.

In Monson's third metaphor, the university is a "mammoth cave," from Plato's account of the educated man's ascent out of the cave into the sunlight. The mammoth cave has many rooms and some areas still unexplored. The faculty are the guides and most of them only know certain parts of the cave. The president is chief guide who has the responsibility to establish and maintain the conditions that will enable others to explore the unknown.

We see how difficult it is to describe the role of president and the conflicting role expectations of each beholder. Each trustee, professor, student, legislator, and donor has a metaphor for the college or university from which flows an image of the way a president is supposed to be!

In the late 1960s and early 1970s, the "crisis-manager," "cool-under-fire," and similar role expectations became commonplace. As the situation changes, role expectations change. (I shall not attempt to portray the lacerating impact of the Vietnam War on the campus.) If the change is swift, as it has been since the early 1970s, presidents may not be able to change quickly enough to satisfy the conflicting perceptions of what is required. I illustrate this by recalling the service of a very good man, called to the presidency of the most tragically torn campus in the country, trying to recover from its trauma of violent protest and student deaths. Responding to the entreaties of a governing board to provide a healing force, the new president was in office less than a month when he was informed of a several million dollar deficit that had to be rectified at once. The people who brought in a diplomat-healer now added to the agenda for the first year the role of retrencher, and tight-fisted money manager. Such is the way of the presidency in difficult times.

Thus, by the mid 1970s, the public image of the president was of a harried, if energetic, executive type rushing through "revolving-door" positions. In early 1975, a feature story in the *Chronicle of Higher Education*, "The Perilous Presidencies" by Philip Semas, described presidential firings and resignations and the disenchantment with higher education among the citizenry and legislatures. Photographs of five recently fired presidents were featured with the story.

In 1976, the annual Special Report of Editorial Projects for Education, Inc., published in hundreds of college and university alumni magazines, used a feature story entitled "The Impossible Job?" It asked who would want to be a president under the conditions that exist, and it recounted the tale of woe of the late 1960s and early 1970s. It ended with a continuing and perplexing question.

> Must tomorrow's college and university presidents, then, be mediators, low-profile crisis managers trained in the arts of conciliation? Apostles of efficiency? Task-oriented—a closed circle of managers revolving from institution to institution as particular needs demand particular talents? (P. 16)

Not too long ago, some observers suggested a division of the presidency into inside and outside parts. That suggestion has not been generally accepted. So the contradictions and complexities of the role continue. People still seek to serve in the 350 or more presidential vacancies that occur each year.

My own experience tells me that the role today contains several dimensions that logically flow from the tasks to be performed. The tasks are not all that different from what they have been over many years. Yet, as the situation changes, effective performance of those tasks requires different skills and competencies.

Presidential Functions

The tasks or functions include, first, leadership, which I separate from management and control. That leadership function is to keep all concerned, both inside and outside constituencies and forces, keenly aware of the central purposes, values, and worth of the higher education enterprise. The president should be what Harlan Cleveland calls "a situation-as-a-whole" person, the one person who does not lose sight of the institution's goals. The president should constantly influence the shaping and reshaping of those goals.

Concomitantly, the president has a representational, communication, and interpretation function that focuses on the value of a college or university being made known to others, crucial to its support and maintenance. Effective relationships between the institution and other key entities are essential to the college's health and well-being. I do not see how responsibility for either leading or communicating can be delegated to others.

The management and control functions are vitally important as well. Although the president is responsible for these, and must be accountable for them, the delegation of such functions to a management team or cabinet is possible and desirable.

In sum, the president is at the center of a vastly complex and fragile human organization. Whatever one chooses as a leadership metaphor—mayor, prime minister, executive, manager—the president must be effective, or the institution will suffer. In this era of anti-institution attitudes, we must remember that institutions were created to protect and transmit something of value to people. Without constant vigilance and renewal, institutions lose that sense of value in the eyes of those citizens they are supposed to serve. The survival of the president is not the goal. The leader is temporary and, if necessary, expendable in service to the potential value of the institution. I do not mean that we should treat presidents harshly. Quite the contrary. Knowing that they will expend themselves in such service, we should honor them more.

3/ Selecting College and University Presidents Today

This chapter is concerned with searching for and selecting college and university presidents. It is intended to aid governing board members, faculty and students who will serve on search committees, and those persons who might have the nerve or courage to permit themselves to become candidates for a presidency. More than that, however, it is an attempt to give the general reader an understanding of the key issues and problems involved in presidential selection. Anyone interested in higher education should understand the presidential selection process, for it illuminates the complexity of both the unique organization a college or university represents, and the governance considerations that flow from that uniqueness.

There are two contemporary books on presidential selection. I wrote *The Selection of College and University Presidents* in 1974, and it has been used widely as a guidebook by search committees. The other guide, *Presidential Search*, published in 1979, was written by John W. Nason, whom I served as consultant in its preparation. I urge readers to examine both these publications in addition to the material that follows for it is my intention to avoid a step-by-step treatment of the search process here. Instead, I want to highlight those aspects of the search and selection process that are particularly troublesome or controversial. My experiences as researcher of the process, and consultant for some searches, have given me some new understandings I wish to share.

Presidential Turnover

Presidential turnover and finding "good" presidents for our colleges and universities have been subjects of interest for a long time. In 1899, when total national enrollment in colleges and universities stood at 140,000, Stimson said:

The fact that some nine or ten (colleges) are in the field searching for presidents, with evident difficulty in finding them, would indicate that there is uncertainty as to just what is wanted, or that the evolution of the requisite type of man has not kept pace with the evolution of the college (p. 451).

The turnover rate is higher today than in the past. In 1935, Greenleaf reported in *School and Society* that there were 133 new college presidents among the 1,662 institutions then in existence, or a turnover rate of approximately 8 percent that year.

The 1976–77 *Education Directory: Colleges and Universities,* prepared by the National Center for Education Statistics, reports 363 presidential changes in postsecondary institutions, or a turnover rate of 12.6 percent for four-year institutions and a 10.8 percent rate for two-year institutions. My monitoring of presidential turnover in the calendar year 1977 showed a total turnover rate of 13 percent.

The 1978–79 *Directory* shows a total turnover rate for postsecondary institutional presidencies of 13.8 percent, plus the entry of a new category of "system" presidencies, with a turnover rate of 17 percent.

There has also been, for some time, speculation over the average number of years served or tenure of presidents. As with the invoking of statistics on any matter, there is not universal agreement on what the figures may mean. Harold Stoke, writing in 1958 (p. 17), said that the average term for college presidents is about four years and if it were not for the exceptional records of some, it would be much shorter.

In 1970, Clark Kerr reported that the "median years of experience" of the Association of American University presidents had decreased from seven years in 1929 to two years in 1969 (pp. 139–40).

Cohen and March (pp. 153–93) devoted a chapter entirely to presidential tenure. They provide considerable data relating length of presidential tenure to the size of the institution, rate of growth of the institution, and age of the president. They show that presidents are much more likely to leave at about age fifty than they are at ages forty-three or fifty-seven. Presidential departures are also keyed to length of service in a way that suggests an implicit term of office that is five years long, with decreasing prospects of renewals. In the spring of 1970, the personal interviews with the presidents were conducted by the authors. When the book reporting on the study was published in 1974, I computed that a total of 45 percent of the forty-two presidents studied were no longer in their jobs!

My own research interviews with thirty-two new presidents completing their first year of service were conducted in 1976. In preparing this book, I re-examined the status of that group. I find that thirteen of the thirty-two are no longer in those presidencies, which is an attrition of some 40 percent over that three-year period.

However one wishes to view these facts and figures, they clearly reveal the need to search for and select a significant number of new chief executive officers each year. They also make clear to me the relatively temporary nature of the presidential role. Rather than judge whether that is good or bad, governing boards should face this fact, provide for it, plan on it, and supply the kind of support and work conditions that should enable their institutions to have outstanding leadership, despite the temporary nature of such posts. (We will return to this subject in chapter eight when we consider the personal side of the presidency.)

Selection in the Past

One observer of the rites of presidential selection has referred to today's style of presidential search as "an Easter egg hunt: many people want to participate, and thousands want to watch" (Hyde, p. 186). Certainly over the past decade, the search process for a college or university president has been drastically altered from one of imperious trustee choice to one that many consider of excessive participation by everybody.

Is the search for a new president a unique opportunity for institutional renewal or a fate to be avoided and bemoaned? I have known some governing board members who tolerated a president's ineptitude far longer than proper in order to avoid the pain and controversy of going through another search process. Why is it so complicated?

We must remember that the roots of American colleges and universities go all the way back to the medieval period and the University of Paris. Existing under the protection and sufferance of the Roman Catholic church, the faculty members were primarily clerics, and many of the students were preparing for clerical roles and offices. Daly tells us that in the thirteenth century four "nations" existed at the university, each somewhat independent of the university, and made up of *masters of arts*. In effect, these were the faculty in the arts, each of the "nations" possessing its own seal, chapels, and places of assembly. The head of each "nation" was called a "proctor." In the fourteenth century, the proctor was elected by each "nation" and served a term of one *month*. Proctors were kept accountable, as representatives of their "nation," by having to stand for monthly election. They represented their nation, not the university.

The rector was the elected faculty member who held the highest office in the university. Daly tells us that the four proctors were authorized to elect the rector who, in the latter part of the thirteenth century, was elected *four times a year*. (The faculty of arts did not delegate its authority very greatly nor for any significant length of time!)

The election of the rector was similar to that of a pope in that the four electors (the proctors) were locked in a special room and forbidden to communicate with anyone outside. A candle of specified length was lighted, and they were to complete the election before the light went out. If the candle burned out before they could make up their minds, then four other electors were to be selected, and the voting began again. Finally, a rector was elected for the next *three-month term*.

I cite this history to show how far we have moved in the time and manner of presidential selection. I make no judgment as to the direction we have taken.

Determining the Search and Selection Process

Given the predictability of presidential turnover, it would seem prudent for each governing board to have provisions in their code or bylaws covering the procedures to be followed in the event of a presidential vacancy. There is usually controversy enough at a time of presidential turnover; trying to create a new procedure at such a time may compound the difficulties. The governing board should be able to turn to its adopted policy and procedures concerning presidential vacancies, without delay.

It should be made clear, whatever the circumstances, that the governing board will determine the process by which any constituent groups participate in selecting a president and that authority for the selection and appointment of the new president rests with the governing board.

Participation

The first issue a governing board will have to decide when establishing a search and selection procedure is that of consultation or participation by faculty and others inside and outside the institution. While there may be initial resentment at the expectations or demands for participation or consultation, an important principle is also to be weighed here: that of the legitimacy of authority or power in a human organization. How does one's authority obtain legitimation without appearing imperious and arbitrary. How does a governing board assure its appointee that the various constituent groups will accept his or her authority and be cooperative— at least at the outset? In my view, the best way to achieve such cooperation is to gain the consensus or support of the various groups through their representation, participation, or consultation in the search process.

In 1970 when Harvard University's Committee on Governance drafted recommendations for the procedures to be used in selecting a new president, it included ways to carry out the most effective consultation process. The committee's memorandum stated:

> The consultation process has a number of purposes. Because questions related to the presidency are complex and not convincingly answerable by any one person, consultation among a wide variety of people should generate useful ideas and answers for those who are charged with

choosing a president. Furthermore, *the Fellows have no intention of choosing a president unacceptable to his constituencies; a sensible process of consultation with these constituencies should help the Fellows achieve this goal* (p. 2, emphasis added).

Put another way, because the president is usually seen as the link between all the constituencies of a university, the involvement of representatives of those constituencies enables the institution to clarify its goals, unite support for objectives and priorities, and select a new leader it can support fully. Failure to provide for these groups' consultation or participation usually results in resentment and in lack of cooperation and commitment to the success of the chosen leader. (I do not, however, have a romantic notion about the ease of consultation or participation. Enabling these groups' participation can sometimes be more difficult than the search process itself.) Despite trustees' and administrators' resistance, almost all colleges and universities now allow for some faculty and, to a much lesser degree, some student participation in searching for and selecting a president.

Presidential Selection Models

Before the search commences, clear ground rules and guidelines should exist in writing. The process can get extremely complex, and one should not create *ad hoc* criteria or procedures. The procedures themselves could thus become the source of controversy and divisiveness.

My own preference is to *separate* the search and screening process from the selection or appointment process. Thus, a search and screen committee, broadly representative of the key constituencies, is enabled to participate in the search for applicants or nominees and in the screening of such persons until the desired number of finalists (or "short list") is reached. The appointing authority then takes over by deciding among the finalists and making an appointment from among them, if possible. If the short list is unacceptable, the search and screen committee must provide additional names.

Some representatives of the governing board should serve on the search and screen committee so that there is maximum communication between all groups represented in the process.

Qualifications—Sense and Nonsense

One of the first duties of a governing board is to develop—preferably in consultation with representatives of constituent groups—a statement of the qualifications to be sought in a new president. Too often such statements are borrowed from other institutions, regardless of similarity, or they become idealistic "philosopher-king" descriptions of unobtainable characteristics. Most often, such lists of qualifications are totally irrelevant to the needs of the institution.

One of my favorite quotations is that of the Yale trustee who is alleged to have commented as follows on the presidential search that ended with the election of President Griswold:

> He had to be a leader, a magnificent speaker and great writer, a good public relations man and fund raiser, a man of iron health and stamina, married to a paragon—a combination Queen Victoria, Florence Nightingale, and best dressed woman of the year—a man of the world, but with great spiritual qualities, an experienced administrator who can delegate authority, a Yale man and a great scholar, and a social philosopher who has at his fingertips a solution to all of the world's problems. I don't doubt that you have concluded that there is only One who has most of these qualifications. But, we had to ask ourselves—is God a Yale man? (Demerath, p. 56).

I have also been struck by the similarity of qualifications sought in presidents and those qualities Aristotle described in *The Rhetoric* as attributes of men "in their prime." He first portrays the Youthful type of character in phrases such as: "They have exalted notions because they have not yet been humbled by life . . . would rather do noble deeds than useful ones." He also portrays the character of Elderly Men, "who are past their prime, sure about nothing, [regard] life on the whole as a bad business . . . too fond of themselves." As for "Men in Their Prime," which Aristotle defines as free of the extremes of either the Young or the Elderly, "they have neither that excess of confidence which amounts to rashness, nor too much timidity, but the right amount of each. They neither trust everybody nor distrust everybody, but judge people correctly."

Aristotle would have suggested selecting presidents who are, regardless of years, "in their prime."

I believe that the qualifications and criteria for the selection should be related to the specific needs of an individual institution or system at a particular point in time. This specificity means that we are identifying situational, rather than personal matters. Each institution must define for itself its current situation, its needs, and prospects. From an assessment of its goals and its situation, the qualifications of its next president will be formulated. Defining its situation, and thus its needs, is a vital task that governing boards must perform, with external assistance if necessary. I do not minimize the difficulty of such a task.

Use of Consultants

A question that usually arises when a presidential vacancy occurs is whether or not to engage a consultant or executive search firm to assist in the task. More private institutions than public employ professional firms or consultants to find a president. However, it is still a minority of institutions that do so.

There are many ways an outside consultant can be of assistance. It is important to know when such help would be of value. If an institution is having difficulty in formulating a description of its situation and leadership needs, an outsider can often raise questions and issues with a governing board or faculty that no one inside that institution can raise. Very often a president has left with acrimony and distrust between the administration and faculty. A way must be found to intervene in the cycle of distrust and a governing board chairman may need outside help for such a purpose.

Sometimes institutions that are relatively young or that have gone through a difficult period, in which the image or reputation of the institution has been damaged, require an outside consultant or firm to help recruit candidates or interpret the new situation to candidates who want someone other than a governing board chairman to respond to their questions. One problem that is very real is getting boards and faculties to make a truthful and candid appraisal of themselves. I find that faculty have a harder time appraising themselves than governing boards. Often faculty members are unrealistic about their institution and the desirability of the presidency of that institution. Sometimes, there is a form of overcompensation operating that seems to exaggerate the qualifications to be sought in an unnecessary, grandiose, and even self-destructive manner.

I have served as a consultant to governing boards of both public and private institutions. For the most part, I have helped boards define what their institutions required of a new president and design a search process that would heal, rather than reopen, wounds in an institution.

If a governing board chooses not to use a consultant, someone within the institution or system must be identified as qualified to deal with nominees and candidates in a knowledgeable and professional way. I recently served as the executive secretary of the University of Wisconsin System Presidential Search Committee. As I communicated with nominees, I found many of them raised questions with me that they were unable to raise with governing board members or, perhaps, faculty members on the search committee. Such questions as the nature of the political situation, the quality of the board, the reasons for the departure of the president, and the like, can be addressed to someone playing the role of interpreter or manager of the selection process.

Within the past year a Presidential Search Consultation Service has been established in Washington, D.C., cosponsored by the Association of American Colleges and the Association of Governing Boards. It also provides names of suitable presidential candidates, in addition to other services related to the search and screening process.

Outside consultants cannot, of course, do the work of the governing board or replace the participation of the institution's key constituencies. Another danger in using such consultants is that some within the institution will resent the obvious influence of "outsiders." In no case can the whole job be turned over to a consultant or firm. But, where necessary, a consultant can help organize the process, speed up the search, identify and evaluate candidates, or even sell a desirable candidate on an institution.

If a board uses a firm or consultant in the search, it should clearly limit the consultant's task. It should make sure that the ambience in the particular institution is understood. Board members should also make sure that they do not wind up purchasing a process that has been used in an entirely different situation. Finally, board members should make sure they retain their full authority to select and appoint the president.

Affirmative Action and the Open Search

Unless some unique circumstances provide a rationale for an inside appointment without a search, I strongly recommend an open national search for presidential vacancies. Legitimation of the authority of a newly appointed president can be difficult if no search was conducted. In addition, an appointment without a search could go against constituent expectations that flow from equal opportunity legislation and affirmative action requirements.

Almost all colleges and universities are covered by provisions of Executive Order 11246, as amended, title VII of the Civil Rights Act, and title IX of the Education Amendments Act of 1972 (Higher Education Act). Public colleges and universities may also have to be responsive to various state regulations in recruitment and hiring.

Obviously, discrimination is prohibited, but legal requirements go beyond that. An institution should be able to provide evidence that, in its recruitment procedures, it has made a meaningful search, attempting to solicit all appropriately qualified applicants, including women and minorities. Thus, resorting merely to "word of mouth" recruiting would be improper.

Many institutions will engage in "affirmative advertising," making clear that women and minorities are welcome to apply. In published notices and advertisements, the description of the presidential opening will contain the phrase, "An Equal Opportunity Employer, M/F." The statement of qualifications for the position should describe the criteria to be used in selecting the new president. Such criteria should not restrict candidates on the basis of race, sex, or age.

With the new requirements, many colleges and universities will use advertisements to demonstrate the openness of their search. Announcements of presidential vacancies are seen frequently in the Sunday edition of the *New York Times* and, especially, in *The Chronicle of Higher Education*. Such advertisements should solicit both nominations and applications. They should briefly describe the institution and qualifications sought for the position and give a deadline date for receipt of names and an address for further correspondence.

In addition to advertising in newspapers, most institutions will want to announce the availability of the position in a variety of other places. Some people overestimate the restrictive nature of affirmative action and equal opportunity requirements. For example, a general announcement or advertisement for a presidential vacancy does not prevent the committee from soliciting nominations and applications from a variety of other sources as well. As long as the same criteria and requirements are used to evaluate all candidates, it is perfectly appropriate and desirable to extend a search beyond those who apply. This expanded search might well include specific solicitation of sources for women and minority, including minority women, candidates. By an "open" search I mean bringing to the attention of all possible interested parties the opportunity to apply or suggest names of persons who should be considered. The requirements, qualifications, and criteria for selection are made clear to all, and there is no secret about the process that will be followed or about the ground rules.

One issue that must be settled at the beginning of a presidential search is confidentiality. Independent colleges and universities can control such matters with relative ease. Public institutions must comply with appropriate state laws. In some states, as will be illustrated later, so-called sunshine laws restrict the ability of the search committee to pledge confidentiality. In Florida and Minnesota, for example, the law permits the press to know names of candidates and to be present when meetings are held to interview and vote on candidates.

There is no question in my mind that the inability of search committee members to pledge confidentiality, at least until the interview stage, prohibits a search from attracting persons who are successful and relatively satisfied with their present positions. Bear in mind, I am speaking of a presidential search; a committee should be able to consider other presidents who, on the basis of experience, might be attracted to move to a different institution. Not being able to guarantee confidentiality is not too serious if a search committee is seeking to attract only persons who have yet to prove themselves in a presidency.

As the process unfolds, however, those candidates remaining on a semifinalist list must be prepared to cooperate in reference and background checks. These semifinalists will be interviewed and a site visit may occur. Although all this activity should be discreet, it is impossible to avoid an awareness of a candidate's involvement at the later stage of a search.

A certain tension is necessary throughout a search. On the one hand, the search process must be seen as open, fair, and rigorous—with the participation of representatives of the key constituencies—aimed at selecting the best possible person for the presidency. The legitimation of the president's authority rests on that goal. On the other hand, an open search is time-consuming and not always gentle, and it risks "turning off" many outstanding people who are successful in excellent posts and do not want to take part in such a contest.

Getting Good Candidates

It has become increasingly difficult, if not impossible, for most institutions merely to seek out an outstanding person and appoint that person as president. Laws, regulations, and bylaws notwithstanding, the expectations of consultation, participation, and a rational search process prohibit such straightforward action. Indeed, the political nature of the presidential role today requires that a person be willing to go through the entire process if he or she wishes to be credible as leader. Nevertheless, there is a serious problem of complexity; governing boards and their search committees must not be defeated by it.

The presidential tradition, going all the way back to the rector of the medieval university, requires that a person be called to the office, rather than apply or campaign for it. The metaphor of candidate is difficult enough. The term "applicant" increases the difficulty. That is why notices of presidential vacancies carry the notation concerning "applications and nominations." It is rare, therefore, to obtain many applications from highly qualified or experienced persons. The style is to arrange for a nomination, if you seek to be a candidate. However, if the search committee does an effective job of contacting knowledgeable people and enlisting their help, nominations and suggestions will be forthcoming for persons who did not initiate the effort and may not be aware of it. Such people may be the most successful in other presidencies and most attractive to the search committee.

My practice has been to advise search committees not to screen and evaluate persons without their knowledge and permission. I prefer to communicate with all persons nominated, informing them of the nature of the position, and the ground rules for the search process, and requesting their permission to allow consideration by submitting a resumé or vita. I also either call nominees or arrange to have them called so that the matter may be discussed further with a knowledgeable representative of the governing board or the search committee. One must encourage promising nominees to become candidates, for there are many aspects of the process, as we have seen, which tend to discourage those who are satisfied and secure in their present positions.

Below are three typical responses from highly successful presidents who were nominated in a recent presidential search, but declined to permit themselves to be considered as candidates:

> I am reluctant to undergo the increasingly complex procedures involved in a search. I appreciate and support many of the reasons for the new search procedures, but I believe that the pendulum has swung too far and that many of these experiences now are unnecessarily burdensome for all concerned.

Another president commented on the "risks" of searches in declining to be seen as a candidate for another presidential position:

> I am concerned with the high risk that would be involved. If you say you are interested or willing to allow your name to be considered, and it becomes known on your campus, you're in trouble! Your faculty, your board, even your staff will want to know, why do you want to leave us, or if you want to, why don't you? All of the relationships become complicated. It's too great a risk to take unless you really do want to get out pretty badly.

One chancellor of a state system said about the problem of searches today:

> Affirmative action and open meeting requirements are construed in such ways today that Boards cannot go out and recruit someone they think would be ideal for the job. Further, experienced and well-placed persons cannot afford to have it become known that they are candidates in a competitive contest. If they are not selected, they have burned their bridges. Thus, many searches tend to end up with relatively undistinguished short lists, of inexperienced people and people in trouble in their present jobs.

Encouraging highly qualified nominees to become candidates is difficult enough without purposefully adding burdens to it. Some search procedures employed seem to be designed to discourage candidates. A search committee may have no control over the provisions of a sunshine law that prohibits confidentiality. But members should guard against a negative tone in their communications and assuming a buyer's market mentality in examining a supposed oversupply of skilled, dedicated, and talented people. Such attitudes are definitely counterproductive. Sometimes, public institutions adopt state personnel selection procedures to find a president and do it badly.

Many institutions use materials in searches that appear to have been ineptly adapted from state or civil service procedures. But most often the institutions that use forms I consider worthy of criticism are parts of state systems and are former teachers colleges. A recent search by Slippery Rock State College in the Pennsylvania State College System demonstrates the point. I think I would rate that system at the low end of a scale on many items, including system of governance, intrusion by state political authorities, and serving as president "at the pleasure of the governor," rather than the board.

During its recent presidential search, the Slippery Rock State College search committee treated everyone as an "applicant." Anyone suggested for the position was required to fill out a formal application for the job if he or she wished to be considered. In addition, each applicant was required to submit transcripts of academic work, four letters of recommendation, a statement describing "your administrative style," and a kind of term-paper in which philosophy and goals would be expressed.

Recruiting good candidates, it seems to me, is a two-way street. Treating the process as one-sided distorts it at the outset. It is not only unwise, it is functionally counterproductive. It is what David Riesman has referred to as "playing one-man chess"; you concentrate only on your moves and strategy, without any thought as to what the other person is thinking, feeling, or doing.

There is no need to force nominees to become applicants and no need for documentation of a person's qualifications until well beyond the first screening. Written references are of limited value anyhow, but requiring them of all applicants is a waste of everyone's time. In summary, search committees should try to put themselves in the candidates' place and plan the search accordingly.

Screening and Assessment of Candidates
Readers are again referred to both my 1974 guidebook and the 1979 Nason guide for specific techniques used in the screening process.

A major problem in searching for a president is the assessment of prior administrative experience and success of candidates. There is an assumption that holding a position for several years means success in that position. Yet we need to find a way to evaluate critically the accomplishments in that position. We are also constantly in danger of the "peter principle." Needed is a way of finding out if we are taking someone out of a job he or she performed competently and placing him or her in a new position in which he or she will be incompetent.

Another problem of the assessment phase of a presidential search often associated with maximum participation of constituent representatives is that all but the timid will be screened out. Those candidates with survival skills, those with "nice" personalities, those who will appease rather than lead, it is feared, are the finalists. Search committee members must be vigilant that getting "nice" people does not become the principal dynamic in the screening and assessment process. That is why I prefer to include governing board members on the search and screen committee and include all constituent representatives in interviews so that candidates cannot pander to one constituency without peril. Nevertheless, I do not minimize the difficulty of finding a leader who satisfies all the various constituencies. Search committee members must constantly revisit the objective of the entire effort: to find the best qualified person to lead the institution or system, given its present situation and needs, in a process that ensures, as far as possible, respect for and cooperation with the new leader.

Politics of Selection

In my experience, the search and screen process can be quite rational, down to the creation of a short list of the appropriate number of finalist candidates. Most governing boards, in their charge to a search committee, will require no fewer than five names from which they are to select a president. It is at this point that the vagaries of personality, chemistry, and the like seem to take over.

Some finalists are more effective in selling themselves. A board member might not like the personality of a finalist. A spouse may cause some concern. A major donor on the governing board may play an undue role or even have veto power with the board. The strongest candidate may have withdrawn, having been offended by some trustee questions. It is difficult to reconstruct what happens and why at this final stage. It is, however, no time for a board to withhold its clear expectations for performance, nor for a finalist to avoid raising questions, the answers to which are crucial determinants of potential effectiveness. (The issue of assessing presidential effectiveness is treated in chapter nine.)

One story will illustrate what can happen in the final stages of the search process. At a small, church-related Protestant college four finalists were interviewed by the committee. The first candidate interviewed was asked for his view on the role of religion in a liberal arts college. In his lengthy response, the candidate volunteered his personal religious views, including the fact that he was raised as a Catholic and that his wife and children were Catholic, although he had no formal membership in any church at present. He also volunteered that he had supported Eugene McCarthy in the previous presidential election. Although he was a very strong candidate, his selection became almost assured when a powerful trustee personally attacked the candidate for his lack of "appropriate religion" for the position. The faculty called a special meeting and voted to inform the board that they supported the appointment of this particular candidate; he was elected shortly thereafter. (Readers acquainted with Mary McCarthy's *The Groves of Academe* will find in this story a familiar theme.) As a faculty member on the search committee said to me later, "any rejection of this candidate would have looked as though it was based on religious or political views!"

Incidentally, after a one-year "honeymoon" period, the sixty faculty

members of this small college were so disenchanted with the president
that they elected to have collective bargaining, with American Association
of University Professors as their agent, much to the chagrin of the board.

Four presidential searches are described here to illustrate how the
unique circumstances and requirements of each institution are reflected
in the conduct of the search. The illustrations include two private universities and two public universities, both operating with collective bargaining and sunshine laws.

Readers will note how governance traditions influence the role of the
faculty in the search. Further, the existence of sunshine laws and experience with faculty collective bargaining have a significant effect on the
process and the outcome.

Mankato State University—Search for a President, 1978–79

The State University System of Minnesota consists of seven institutions, each headed by a president. The system head is a chancellor with
a central administration staff located in the capitol city, St. Paul. There
is a ten-member State University Board responsible for governing the
system. (The system is separate from the University of Minnesota.)

The faculty and staff work under collective bargaining agreements
negotiated on a systemwide basis. In addition, a state law requires that
all meetings be open to the public. By applying, all candidates for the
presidency waive any right to confidentiality of application material and
credentials.

Qualifications. The statement of qualifications sought for the president
of Mankato State University in 1978 follows:

1. Commitment to role of a public, multi-purpose, regional university
2. Commitment to and understanding of the centrality of teaching and
   scholarship in the educational process
3. Knowledge of educational theories, trends, ideas and resources
4. Ability and commitment to provide effective management
   leadership in a university operating within a collective bargaining
   situation, including:
   • knowledge of and respect for principles of objectivity and due
     process
   • acceptance of the collective bargaining model
   • style characterized by integrity and openness
   • ability to select and work with an effective management team
5. Sophisticated inter-personal skills and sensitivities required to relate
   to many publics and to coordinate functions and members of the
   University community
6. Ability and commitment to communicate ideas and information
   clearly, concisely, and effectively in written and oral form and in
   formal and informal settings

7. Understanding of and commitment to the role of students and faculty in policy making
8. Highly developed analytical and problem-solving skills
9. College-level teaching experience
10. Evidence of increasingly responsible administrative experience
11. Competence in management of fiscal affairs and in planning

Each person interested in being considered was required to complete an application form and to submit "at least" five letters of reference addressed specifically to the eleven qualification criteria listed above.

Search and Selection Process. Responsibility for the conduct of the presidential selection process was in the chancellor's office, with the vice chancellor specifically designated as the person to conduct all correspondence, receive and maintain all records, and schedule and conduct all interviews. No campus-wide search committee was created as there had been during the previous search in 1973, before the faculty organized for collective bargaining.

Preliminary screening of candidates was performed by the vice chancellor and staff. After this screening, the vice chancellor submitted to the chancellor ten to twenty names. The dossiers of these candidates were made available "for review" to selected members of the chancellor's staff, the administrative officers of Mankato State University, and a screening committee composed of eight members and chaired by the vice chancellor: two faculty, two students, two staff, and one alumni representative. They saw only the materials on the candidates presented to them by the chancellor. (During the 1978–79 search, the faculty union refused to participate in or designate representatives for this screening.) The names of persons being considered were announced at that time in a news release from the chancellor's office.

After reviewing comments about the candidates and following further screening by the chancellor's office, the vice chancellor, in consultation with the chancellor, invited three to five candidates to Mankato State University for separate interviews with each of the constituent groups. The groups were limited to ten persons each. (The faculty union refused to participate in the interviews.) There was also an opportunity for alumni and local citizens to meet the candidates. Comments were solicited by the vice chancellor for use in the evaluations. These candidates were interviewed by the chancellor and the senior system staff members in St. Paul.

The chancellor then selected three finalists to be interviewed by the board. This session and the vote were open. Each candidate was assigned a host and was brought into the board room for a three-quarters- to one-hour interview with the board. After the three finalists had appeared, the chancellor made a recommendation to the board, and the board voted. The person elected was called back into the board room, notified of the decision, and a press conference commenced. Margaret R. Preska, vice president for academic affairs at Mankato, was elected president.

Florida Technological University—Search for a President, 1977–78

Florida Tech is a relatively new institution (later renamed University of Central Florida). It opened in 1968 and now has an enrollment of 10,000 students. It is part of the nine campus State University System of Florida, governed by the Florida Board of Regents. It is headed by a president who reports to the board through the chancellor of the system.

There is systemwide faculty collective bargaining by the American Federation of Teachers, the faculty bargaining agent. In addition, there is an unusually strong sunshine law which I believe has a significant effect on the presidential search and other matters related to governance. Any person who wished to be considered for the presidency of Florida Tech was informed that, under the provisions of the Florida sunshine law, "all Search Committee meetings will be open to the public *and all records, résumés and related data available for public inspection*" (emphasis added).

Qualifications and Criteria. The Florida Tech search used a screening process consisting of three separate evaluations of candidates. First, all candidates' résumés were evaluated against a six-item list of minimum selection criteria. Candidates meeting such criteria were advanced and then evaluated on an eight-item list of second-round criteria. Only those who survived the second-round evaluations were considered for further background checks and campus interviews. The minimum selection criteria of the first round and the second-round criteria (FTU Presidential Search Advisory Committee, 1978) are listed below:

Minimum Selection Criteria. In order to be considered further, a person should meet each of the following criteria or equivalent.

1. Terminal Degree—must hold an earned Doctorate from an accredited institution in a recognized academic discipline.
2. Academic Administrative Experience—must have a minimum of five years of experience in a responsible academic administrative position (e.g., department chairman or higher).
3. Overall Academic and/or Professional Experience—must have a minimum of ten years of academic and/or professional experience in at least two permanent positions at separate institutions. To fulfill this requirement, at least one appointment must have been in a tenure earning capacity at a college or university.
4. Specific Academic Qualifications—must have served as a classroom teacher at the rank of instructor or higher and provide evidence of scholarly achievement.

5. Academic Rank—must hold or have held the rank of associate professor or higher.
6. Community Relations—must show evidence of community involvement.

Second Round Presidential Selection Criteria:
A. A history of successful teaching or scholarly achievement in higher education.
B. Demonstrated superior administrative skills and a belief in the concept of delegation of appropriate authority and responsibility among administrative, academic, student and faculty units.
C. Must show evidence or express the sincere belief that the overriding, major goal of the university is the education of its students; socially and emotionally, as well as academically.
D. Ability to foster a common purpose and commitment through a respect for and willingness to work cooperatively with students, faculty, staff and alumni.
E. Ability to represent effectively the role of the University in the state education system, and to express that role to the various publics and thus attain their confidence and gain their moral, political, and financial support.
F. Be a person of intellectual and personal integrity, open to divergent opinions and ideas but able and willing to act decisively when the need arises.
G. Demonstrated good health and sufficient mental and physical energy to cope with the demands placed upon him/her by the university constituents.
H. A demonstrated sensitivity, understanding and commitment to affirmative action, equal access and equal opportunity programs.

Search and Selection Process. When Charles Millican resigned as president of Florida Tech on May 2, 1977, the Board of Regents of the State University System of Florida appointed a three-person regents search committee to coordinate the search and to recommend a person to be named president. This committee, in turn, established an FTU presidential search advisory committee, representative of the campus, and charged it with responsibility for conducting the actual search and screen functions and for recommending at least three finalists.

The advisory committee consisted of thirteen persons, chaired by the acting president of FTU. The members of the committee represented each of the six college faculties, the staff, alumni, and the student government.

Because the records and minutes of the search are open to the public, it is possible to recapitulate the results of each screening procedure. Of the 174 original nominations and applications, a total of sixty-three persons passed the initial screening. Applying the second-round evaluation criteria, the advisory committee reduced the list to twenty candidates.

Following background checks, the committee invited eight persons (and spouses) to Florida Tech for interviews. Two-and-one-half-day interview schedules were arranged for each of the eight candidates. Interview questions were prepared in advance, each candidate had an assigned sponsor from the committee; and interview schedules included visits with various constituencies of the university, the local community, the chancellor, as well as the advisory committee. Also planned were interview schedules for the spouses, who in this case were all women.

Following the interviews, the advisory committee reduced the list by vote to five persons. One candidate received all affirmative votes, the other four received a majority of affirmative votes. The list of the five finalists, along with the voting tallies and dossiers, was transmitted to the Board of Regents search committee. That committee interviewed all five finalists, and on January 9, 1978, unanimously recommended the highest ranked candidate, Dr. Trevor Colbourn, to the full Board of Regents for election to the presidency.

Tulane University—Search for a President, January 15, 1974–January 3, 1975

Tulane University of Louisiana, located in New Orleans, is a major independent university of approximately 10,000 students. Its schools and colleges include law, medicine, engineering, and other professional schools, in addition to arts and sciences. It is governed by a board of administrators. Herbert E. Longenecker was to retire on July 1, 1975, following fifteen years of service as president of Tulane University.

Qualifications and Criteria. The board did not attempt to draw up a formal set of qualifications and characteristics required of a new president. Rather, it included a statement in its material soliciting nominations as follows.

> In developing a list of nominees, the Presidential Search Committee does not intend to prescribe an inflexible set of specifications with respect to the qualifications and background of the potential candidates but will naturally expect that they be persons of highest integrity and character, experienced in education, business, or government, and possessing the desire and the ability to assume the leadership of a venerable and highly respected private institution. The nominee should be a person with sound philosophy of higher education aimed at academic excellence.
>
> Tulane, like all privately endowed educational institutions, is faced with the necessity of developing additional financial resources from external sources. Thus, the new President of Tulane University should be able to represent the University's case to the public and possess the experience, aptitude, and interest in order to develop new and additional resources for the institution.

Search and Selection Process. Upon acceptance of the resignation of President Longenecker, the board authorized the chairman to appoint a committee to aid in the selection of a new president. The board resolution stated that participation would include representatives from the faculty, students, and alumni of the university. A meeting of the representatives of the various constituent groups with the board chairman led to the creation of a "Committee to Engage in the Identification of Candidates from Among Whom the Board of Administrators Shall Choose the Next President of Tulane University." This committee was then referred to as the Presidential Search Committee.

The search committee was made up of ten members: two board members, selected by the board; one administrative officer, selected by the president; two alumni, selected by the alumni association; three faculty members, selected by the faculty senators of the university senate; and two students to be selected by the student senate. In addition, each of the constituent groups associated with the university was encouraged to provide suggestions and nominations to the committee.

The committee elected one of the board members as its chairman and designated the administrator (Dr. Clarence Scheps, executive vice president) as the secretary of the committee.

Two further matters were decided by the committee in developing their procedures: (1) members decided that, "utilizing confidential procedures similar to those currently employed for selection of candidates for Honorary Degrees, [the committee] shall obtain the advice and consent of the Faculty Senators of the University Senate"; and (2) the committee would submit an alphabetically arranged list of acceptable candidates to the board of no fewer than three nor more than ten.

Of 265 names considered by the committee, twelve were chosen for on-site interviews. The chairman of the committee participated in all the site visits, as did the chairman of the board, plus at least two of the faculty members. Detailed reports of these interviews were made to the full committee which voted to reduce the list to eight persons.

The eight names, with full background material, were submitted to the thirty-two elected members of the faculty senate (of the university senate). Following a veto procedure similar to that used in the advise and consent process for honorary degree candidates, the faculty senate approved five of the candidates. (Note the significant role given to the faculty of this university, which would have been considered highly inappropriate at either Mankato State University or Florida Tech.)

The board invited each of the five finalists to the university for interviews and, on December 5, 1974, voted to invite Dr. Francis Sheldon Hackney to become president. The chairman and vice chairman of the board went to Dr. Hackney's home, in Princeton, New Jersey, to confer with him, and on January 2, 1975, Dr. Hackney accepted the offer.

University of Denver—Search for a Chancellor, 1977–78
The University of Denver (Colorado Seminary) is the oldest and largest

independent educational institution between the Midwest and west coast. Founded in 1864, the university has an enrollment of approximately 8,000 students. It is governed by a board of trustees. Chancellor Maurice B. Mitchell announced his resignation on November 28, 1977. He had served for approximately ten years.

Qualifications and Criteria. The board, following the guidance in *The Selection of College and University Presidents* (Kauffman, 1974), stated that the selection criteria for the new chancellor should be related to the specific needs of the University of Denver:

> The University of Denver is at a critical stage of its development. It has recently adopted a statement of goals committing itself as a private independent university to learning, research and scholarship. It further states that we are dedicated to intellectual and cultural pursuits, no matter whether these pursuits be professional or liberal in character. Of the many University goals, the most characteristic to be singled out would be that combination of liberal and specialized education which prepares students for ultimate entry into professional life.
>
> The University has also embarked upon a major capital fund drive to provide the economic base for the accomplishment of its stated goals. This fund drive is just getting underway and it will be a major determinate of the University's future development.
>
> Thus, two major areas are critical in assessing the leadership qualities needed in the new Chancellor—one a deep commitment to and demonstrated experience in scholarly pursuits and academic affairs; the other, successful administrative experiences and community relations to provide guidance to the development of the economic base of the University. Along with these qualities, candidates for Chancellor must be reviewed for the necessary personal traits that provide the basic skills involved in good human relations.
>
> More specifically, the following criteria are suggested for the review of all candidates:
>
> 1. *Demonstrated scholarly competence including the earned doctorate or its equivalent.* Scholarly competence is measured not only in earned degrees. We should be looking for people who have written or spoken on significant scholarly subjects. While an earned doctorate is not a requirement, it would be highly desirable for the candidate to have undergone the academic discipline represented by the doctorate.
> 2. *Experience in a university setting related to education, including serving on educational boards and commissions.* Preferably a candidate should have had some experience in a university setting. This could include serving on task forces, commissions, boards of trustees or other education-related organizations.
> 3. *Successful administrative experience that clearly demonstrates leadership capacity in financial management.* The University of Denver is a $42 million corporation. The Chancellor, as chief executive officer, must have competence in providing leadership in effective and efficient financial management.

4. *Broad understanding of Academic Affairs as related to long-range planning and implementation.* What we are looking for here is a genuine understanding and respect for the role of higher education in American society.
5. *Exceptional facility in Human Relations.* Candidates should possess skills in involving their colleagues in cooperative efforts that would be helpful in maintaining a rich and stimulating organization.
6. *Evidence of Productive Community Relations including governmental relations and fund-raising.* Candidates should be able to present the University of Denver to friends and potential friends convincingly. They should have ability to lead in developing an organized program of activities to produce the necessary financial support for a program of quality education. This includes contacts not only with the business community but with local, state, and federal governments.
7. *Personal traits necessary for the most exacting executive responsibilities.* Obviously, we would want candidates with intelligence, integrity, a sense of humor, maturity and vigor, and a capacity for hard work and good health. These are not easily discernible in written material but should be factors to be considered in appointing a top candidate.

Search and Selection Process.   The board of trustees made clear to all at the outset that they had the responsibility for selecting and appointing a new chancellor. The president of the board was empowered to appoint a six-person Trustees' Chancellor Selection Committee. That committee was authorized to start soliciting nominations. It was chaired by Trustee Walter Koch.

Also authorized was a ten-person University Advisory Committee, to include two representatives of the alumni, four faculty, one undergraduate student, one graduate student, one staff person, and a chairperson to be designated by the board. (The chairperson was Kenneth W. Kindelsperger, associate vice chancellor for academic affairs; he had recently led a successful search for a new dean at the law school.) Leaders of the various constituent groups were requested to nominate more persons than would be appointed so that the advisory committee would be representative and would include women and minorities.

The dominant committee was the trustee committee, although the advisory committee members participated in screening and evaluating candidates. Due to the effectiveness of the advisory committee chairman, the committees fully cooperated in the screening process. In addition, the services of the Presidential Search Consultation Service (PSCS), affiliated with the Association of American Colleges, were used to obtain names of promising candidates.

The pool of approximately 150 people was reduced primarily through examination of written materials. The committees, meeting jointly, re-

duced the list to approximately fifteen persons and, then, through telephone checking, reduced it still further to six persons. All six persons
(including two inside candidates) were interviewed, but only by members
of the two committees, meeting separately. At the conclusion of the
interviews, each committee ranked the candidates.

Since there was unanimous agreement on the first choice of both
committees, that candidate and his spouse were invited back to the campus
for a full, three-day schedule of meetings with trustees, faculty, administrators, students, alumni, and community leaders. Systematic feedback
was sought, through the various constituent representatives on the advisory committee. Although some faculty objected to having no one to
compare the candidate with, and preferred to see others, the selection
committee recommended Dr. Ross Pritchard to become the fourteenth
chancellor and the Board of Trustees so voted.

A key role was played by the advisory committee chairman, who
served as an effective liaison between the faculty and the trustees. Without
his effectiveness, campus constituent groups might have resisted more
strongly the design of the search process.

Summary
It would be far less frustrating and certainly less time-consuming if a
board could select a person to be president without extensive consultation.
The quality of persons thus selected would, in my opinion, be as high as
those now selected. However, both the expectations of constituent groups
and various legal or moral requirements have brought us to a process of
participation and consultation with persons not on the governing board.
While some presidential candidates might prefer to avoid the competitive
process and the "auditioning," most are aware that the political nature
of institutional leadership today requires some constituent involvement.
A disdain for such participation might indicate a temperament unsuited
for the realities of campus leadership.

I will not, however, express my unqualified approval of what occurs
in many searches. There is such a thing as excessive participation, by
which the selection of the most suitable, qualified president is lost sight
of as the goal, and the politics of representation and the status of participation become ends in themselves. I have seen faculty representatives
exercise a veto because a candidate has not published anything scholarly
lately, or has a degree in a field considered too "applied," or is not
supportive of faculty unions. There is nothing magical about participation,
and constituent representatives may be more close-minded, less generous,
and more self-serving than a governing board they like to portray as
Establishment in their orientation.

Nevertheless, a new leader cannot be imposed, despite legal authority in the hands of the governing board. It is not necessary to use any of the specific selection methods or procedures I have described here. But it is necessary to select a new leader in a manner that will be acceptable to the people who must cooperate and support that new leader. As with democracy, it is messy, often wasteful of energy, and it can be frustrating. However, I do not know of anything better to recommend.

4/ The New College President

As a former college president and as a researcher of the selection process, I have long been interested in what people expect in presidents. I have been struck by the contradictory nature of those expectations.

Most presidential aspirants have some sense of those contradictions when they are going through the selection process but in their eagerness to win the competition, such matters are deferred, if not repressed. After all, if you listen to the questions asked by various constituent representatives it becomes apparent that there are many conflicting expectations. A candidate who only pays attention to the governing board does not usually avoid these conflicts either; it is rare for there to be an absence of divisiveness among board members in priorities and goals.

My initial research was concerned with the search and selection process. To reconstruct the way successful candidates experienced that process, I interviewed a number of newly appointed presidents. (Someone should attempt to study the experience of *unsuccessful* candidates if a way could be found to identify them and enlist their cooperation.) I found new presidents eager and willing to talk in confidence with someone who understood their frustrations. Some were relieved to find out that their own initial experiences in the presidency were not unique or due to some flaw in their own judgment or competence.

In the academic year 1976–77, I conducted a study of thirty-two college and university presidents who were completing their first year in the presidency (Kauffman, 1977; Kauffman and Walker, 1978). Through personal interviews I gathered material related to the disparity between expectations and realities of the college presidency. My object, in all my research and writing, is to find ways better to describe the realities of the presidency in higher education. While at times I may concentrate on problems and difficulties, I do not intend to desanctify the prestige or aura surrounding this vital institutional role. Quite the contrary, my aim is to increase the effectiveness of the presidency by conveying greater understanding of its actual nature and complexity, for I believe that effective presidencies are essential to the life of our colleges and universities.

What follows, herein, are my thoughts on the problems confronted by new presidents, drawn from those previous interviews, and my further work and thought since then.

Why No School?

It may seem to be surprising that a higher educational enterprise that provides preparation for almost every known profession or vocation, and some that are just developing, does not also provide comparable preparation for college presidents. For the most part, a governing board that is weighing a candidate for the office is assessing performance in a previous administrative assignment, not a presidency. There is, therefore, a certain amount of "on-the-job training" that occurs.

Stoke (pp. 13–14) pointed out that there is no school for training future members of Congress, either. He observed that, as with the college president, "the processes of selection are too capricious, the chances of selection too remote." I must also observe that the presidency is a temporary role. Presidents, as with some congressmen, may serve for a long time, but it seems difficult to plan one's entire adult life around the expectation of such a profession or career. Thus, just as some lawyers become, temporarily, congressmen, and some bankers become bank presidents, some economists become deans, and some historians become college presidents. Their principal identity often lies with their profession and not with their temporary office, as important and consuming as that may be.

Since World War II, the academic study of higher education has developed as an applied field. Although most college presidents have not studied or obtained degrees in higher education or in a field of administration, such programs are becoming increasingly important for the preparation of middle-level administrators, especially in areas such as planning, evaluation, budgeting, institutional research, and student affairs. Most presidents do not view such programs as relevant to the presidency because those who teach in such programs rarely have the appropriate experience to maintain credibility with presidents.

I head a doctoral program in such a higher education department now, and I am mindful that it would be almost impossible to create a curriculum that would prepare a person for the presidency. Nevertheless, a body of knowledge and practice is building, and it is increasingly useful for senior-level college and university administrators.

For the most part, then, new presidents obtain whatever may pass for "training" in various institutes and seminars they may attend *after* their appointment. Often, these take place a year following their assumption of office since the classes are usually scheduled in the summer. The Office of Leadership Development of the American Council on Education (ACE) sponsors institutes for both new and veteran presidents. The American Association of Junior and Community Colleges (AAJCC) is involved in a variety of leadership training programs. Some university centers of higher education sponsor workshops appropriate to the needs of college and university presidents. On the whole, however, it must be said that there is little schooling for the job.

All the more reason then for each governing board of an institution, or system, to provide some purposeful orientation for new appointees. I found such orientation rarely occurred. On the whole I found that following a painstaking search and great involvement of board members, new presidents were left, often feeling abandoned, to figure out for themselves what the job was all about.

More than a decade ago, a New York State Regents Advisory Committee on Educational Leadership presented a report and recommendations on the role of the president (1967). It was aimed at improving the effectiveness of those who lead New York's colleges and universities, but its recommendations are germane to all. Briefly, in a section on the induction of new presidents, the report recommends that the new president should be aided and encouraged to visit similar types of institutions before taking office. The new president should also spend time, informally, with trustees, faculty, students, and alumni, before formally assuming his or her duties. Such an orientation is seen as crucial to understanding the environment of a campus before being confronted with specific problems that require action.

Conferring Legitimacy

A new president gains authority in part through public confirmation of his appointment, which is a matter of informing various people and constituencies about the facts of the selection and appointment. It is assumed that the governing board, having selected a president, has notified all other finalist candidates that the search process has come to its end and expressed its gratitude to those who have been willing to cooperate in the process. As a courtesy, the search committee members and leaders of the various constituent groups should be notified of the choice immediately before the public announcement of the new president. Except in those few cases where the press is present at the selection vote, release of information to the press and other public relations activities related to the appointment should be carefully planned and well coordinated. Much is communicated about the status of the office by the manner in which the presentation of the new president is handled.

Public institutions may want to notify the governor and other key state officials before the public announcement is made. Careful thought should be given to the public announcement so the process does not collapse at the end because of leaks to the press and the like.

The question of presidential inauguration will also have to be addressed. Many independent institutions use the occasion to conduct a full-scale celebration, bringing together alumni leaders, benefactors, and the entire college community as a support-building device. It can be both functional and ceremonial. Some public institutions no longer conduct inauguration ceremonies, particularly those in multicampus systems where turnover may be frequent. However, public colleges and universities may find it of great value to use the appointment of a new president to educate the public of the board's agenda and the president's goals. Each institution has to decide what is appropriate for its special needs and situation.

Whatever a board decides on a ceremony or the scale of that ceremony, it is of great importance that the leadership selection process concludes with the formal conferring of legitimacy and sanctioned authority on the new president. The governing board's authority to appoint the president has just been exercised. The president functions under the authority delegated by the governing board. If those familiar words recited by the president at commencement, "by the authority vested in me," are to have full meaning, that vested authority should be given in a meaningful way.

A new president should not have to sneak into town and have people wonder who he or she is, and what he or she is up to. The job is too difficult as it is without adding the burden of questionable legitimacy.

The New Leader and Role Expectations
The metaphors for the useful concepts of role theory are from the stage and the theater. Shakespeare, in *As You Like It,* uses the metaphor to describe the experience of life: "All the world's a stage . . . and one man in his time plays many parts. . . ." When actors portray a part in a play, they take a certain role that is defined in the script, which is their guide, as are the director and the actor's experience in similar parts. If the audience has seen the play many times, they may have preconceptions as to the way the role should be played. Certainly, such ideas will be the basis of the audience's judgment of the quality of the actor's performance.

I find "role" an appropriate concept for attempting to describe the existential nature of a new president's experience. In part, the expectations about the new president's performance in the role will be determined by social norms, rules, differing perspectives, the performances of previous presidents, and especially, by the actor's perception of the expectations of those who observe and react to the performance. The type of institution, its history, traditions, and ethos will also determine many of the role expectations.

The new president may quickly experience unease from the correct perception that the "audience" has inconsistent and contradictory standards and expectations. The other actors on the stage, who were not "auditioned" in the same way, may also have conflicting expectations and give cues in a distracting or disturbing manner.

New presidents often have a sense of exultation about their having been chosen, in a competitive process, which leads to exaggerated notions about their power to achieve great and good things. Sarason (1972) has written skillfully of the dynamics of the new-leader situation and of the socialization of the new leader, who tends to view the experiences in the new setting in the most personal and protective terms.

In many cases, it becomes apparent to the new president that he or she was selected to solve problems, but that moving to solve the problems creates new ones. Often, faculty and staff of a college or university are very ambivalent about finding solutions and accepting the changes that go with them. Every expression of desired change is seen as a criticism of those who did things in the past, and the new leader is not appreciated. If the resistance to change is loud and becomes public, the new president becomes aware that problems, rather than solutions, are being attributed to him or her. The complexity of presidential power is soon appreciated when the governing board inquires how the new president is doing.

The so-called honeymoon period then is often not as blissful as one might imagine. Being looked over in accordance with others' role expectations and labeled as a good or poor "fit" can be disconcerting. Treading carefully to discover the quicksand, the influential opinion-molders on the faculty, those who can be trusted, those with good judgment, and the like is difficult, requiring patience, restraint, and modesty. Sometimes it is difficult to exercise these traits in the new-found role of leader.

There seems to be a deep personal need for the new president to display an attitude of everything's going just great—the governing board made a good decision in selecting me; I made a good decision in coming here as president; this is really a great experience. Nevertheless, I found among the presidents I interviewed relief that they could express reservations and some dismay to someone who would not hold it against them if they revealed that everything was not one hundred percent okay.

The new president readily admits that knowing all about the job of president is very different from experiencing it.

The Role of One's Predecessor

In all but a new institution, a newly appointed president is replacing a predecessor and inheriting that predecessor's form of organization and staff. In addition, the governing board's definition of the institution's situation probably cited a need to redress some imbalance caused by the previous president. All these conditions cause significant problems for the new president.

First, you inherit an administrative organization established previously. In public institutions, the executive and legislative branches of state government may have to approve any alteration of titles or changes in tables of organization. At the very least, the governing board members will have to approve changes in what they had previously thought was an appropriate form of organization. Further, those affected by any changes proposed by a new president will reflect their feelings within their various spheres of influence.

For example, I have known of new presidents who inherit a situation in which all administrative staff report to the president. Such a situation results in an impossible span-of-control problem in which the president becomes the "bottleneck" or stays at the desk all day long dealing with individual administrators. Any attempt to correct such a problem means deciding who reports directly to the president and who reports instead to someone below the president. Since reporting to the president confers status on one, any alteration in this form of organization is seen as demoting persons. Those so "demoted" cannot be expected to appreciate the change in their status, no matter how it is explained.

Often there is a president's advisory committee or council. It, too, may be a measure of status. Sometimes, forty to fifty persons may be on these committees, which are thus totally nonfunctional. Yet attempts to reduce the number are seen as malevolent by some.

I have also seen the obverse of a span-of-control problem. One new university president I know inherited a form of administrative organization in which only one person reported to him. This institution is a large, major complex university in which his predecessor, in the late 1960s era of unrest, insulated himself by the creation of an executive vice-president to whom all other officers reported. When the new president arrived, he found it necessary to "demote" just one person, but then came the problem of deciding who would be given the status of reporting directly to the president.

In addition to the form of organization, a new president inherits a staff. Unfortunately, there is no tradition of presidential appointees resigning when a new president is selected. Thus, one's senior staff, on whom you must rely for judgment, may be unknown to you, may have supported another candidate for the presidency, or the senior staff member may even have been an unsuccessful candidate for the presidency. (Frequently, that last possibility is the case with vice-presidents for academic affairs when an outsider is selected.)

One new chancellor I interviewed had served as acting president at his former university, where he had been provost. He had been an unsuccessful candidate for the presidency of that institution and knew the hurt of that experience. In his new position as chancellor of another institution, he found that the vice chancellor he inherited was an unsuccessful candidate for the post. The vice chancellor had also served as acting chancellor during the search and was eager to play the role of mentor to the new chancellor. Obviously the new chancellor found this situation painful and told me of his agony in seeing this "insider" watching him, sometimes opposing him and judging him. He wished the board had taken care of this problem before he arrived.

Another new university president complained bitterly about the administrative staff members and their attitudes, and he contrasted his own enthusiasm with their cynicism and passivity. However, he also observed, "I guess they have been burned so many times by the bureaucracy of this state they don't want to fight the system as I do."

Sarason describes the experiences of a new leader in a traditional organization and, although he is not necessarily speaking of presidents, I find it most appropriate for this context.

> My education began the first week. I spent the better part of two days
> visiting offices and filling out forms to make sure *I* was on board. . . .
> People were friendly but disinterested. No one was putting out for me. I
> had lunch each day with a different person, on my initiative. In subtle but
> unmistakable ways I was told that there were a bunch of bastards
> running around and some of them might not like me—in fact two of them
> had wanted my job. I felt uneasy, questioned myself about how I had
> misperceived the atmosphere, and I was angry and scared. I came
> floating in on a silver cloud and when I hit the ground, I was hurt (p.
> 199).

Even if one wishes to replace the staff one inherits and you find a basis for obtaining their resignations or discharging them, you are not really free to select a new person on your own. A selection process, not as complex as the president's, but involving an open search, will have to be followed. It could take considerable time, and you may be able only to select from those who are willing to undergo such a search process and can survive it.

By the end of the first year, some new presidents, aware of all the difficulties of releasing people and recruiting and trying to move new people into positions, lower their sights. They find it easier to try to "convert" the inherited staff to new ways than to replace them.

As for redressing the imbalance caused by one's predecessor, I speak of both substance and style. Where there was mistrust between the faculty and administration, a new president is sought to restore trust and harmony. Where an emphasis on harmony has resulted in a reluctance to retrench or remove a budget deficit, a new president is sought who will bring strong management controls to the institution. Obviously, if retrenchment causes a great deal of protest and ill will, the board might fault the president for poor human relations skills. And so it goes.

Whatever the situation, the new president will be compared and contrasted with the predecessor; often his or her agenda, in the first year, will be dominated by the predecessor frame of reference. Such domination sometimes comes as a surprise.

On Being Seen as a Nice Person

One interesting problem seems mostly to beset those who are selected from within an institution to assume the presidency. Often such persons are deans, vice-presidents, or executive assistants to the president. They are known, usually liked, admired, and trusted for their openness, accessibility, discretion, and for their influence with the president. They take great pride in the sound relationships they have established with the faculty and staff. They enjoy the influence which has come about from being able to get answers from an aloof and inaccessible president. Most of all, they are proud of their image and reputation as a "good guy" in an administration that may be portrayed quite negatively and harshly.

On assuming the presidency, such popular persons often experience great anguish in the reality of their new role. It is one thing to be available as a vice-president to anyone who wanted to talk. One could be sympathetic without having to act. It is quite another thing to be as available or neutral as president.

One new president had served for several years as the executive vice-president at his university before assuming the presidency. He commented,

> I was a buffer for the president. I was accessible when the president was not. I was the person who would listen to those who wanted to complain and bring problems. Now I don't have such a buffer for myself, and everyone still wants to see me personally. Many of those who were used to dropping by to chat with me informally now perceive me as the old friend who is too busy to see them or care about them. I find it uncomfortable to be regarded as distant, and I am also disturbed by the naïveté of the faculty and staff who think it can be the same. I need to develop the organization and staff to siphon off some of this, but I still feel I want to be accessible. I confess that I had not anticipated this problem sufficiently.

Another new president in a large public institution had served as faculty member and dean for many years. His father had been a member of the faculty as well, and he and his family had all graduated from the institution. Therefore, everyone knew him, and he knew everyone connected with the institution, including the board members. He described his predecessor as a highly autocratic person who had been in office for more than twenty years.

The only problem I had was finding a way to see all my friends who want to come by and see me. When I was Dean everyone used to come and see me with their problems and I would try to settle them. I enjoyed that. Now I find that I have inherited a staff that was not used to taking any responsibility or initiative because they were afraid of the previous president. Now I find I have to see a lot of people who want to talk to me. *After* listening to them, I have to tell them to see the appropriate administrator on my staff. Then I have to see that administrator first to tell them that I want them to handle the matter . . . it's a problem.

The need for a strong and affirmative self-concept is vital for anyone in a pressure-packed job such as chief executive officer of an institution. One needs to bring that strength to the position and not be dependent on others' views of whether or not you are a decent person of integrity. Sometimes insiders experience a shock in having people they thought of as friends and admirers turn into critics or opponents. Such changes can be serious enough to cause considerable self-doubt and anguish.

The Time Problem
New presidents report that their first year's experience is exhausting, that they feel burned-out, and wonder how they will be able to maintain such a schedule year after year. The pace and the problems seem relentless. No matter how many hours are spent in work, it seems there is always something important remaining to be done. They vow to either get more help or reshape the job "next year."

The writing about executives in the business world often refers to the problem of time and time management. Peter Drucker (p. 79), respected management expert, has observed that "any job that has defeated two or three men in succession, even though each had performed well in his previous assignments, must be assumed unfit for human beings. It must be redesigned. . . . Our experience [with university presidencies finds] only a small minority of the appointments to this position work out—even though the men chosen have almost always a long history of substantial achievement in earlier assignments."

New presidents tend to feel that they have no basis for judging what requires their time and what does not. The invitations to speak and to attend various social and ceremonial occasions arrive. The decision to accept almost all invitations is based on the rationale that one is new and should not offend anyone. After making the rounds one time, it is thought, we can decline a second invitation. Everyone wants to meet with the new president and get acquainted or, better still, acquaint him or her with one's favorite projects, complaints, or items that were turned down by the previous president. How do you know who or what to turn down, in advance? Do you want to make up your own mind about people and projects, or take the view of others who may have a stake in maintaining the status quo? At the beginning one tries to be generous and accommodate everyone. It can be killing.

Warren Bennis (pp. 16–28) has commented on this phenomenon. He writes:

> What happens to top men—and I think that men and women who are *new* to the burdens of high position are specially vulnerable because they are trying to prove themselves—is that they end up with a kind of battle fatigue, overworked, acting as policemen and/or ombudsmen and, what's worse, seriously undermining the legitimacy and effectiveness of the other executives reporting to them (p. 16).

In another passage that I find especially poignant, Bennis refers to the mistake of taking on too much in trying to prove oneself and observes that "we collude, as it were, in the unconscious conspiracy to immerse us in routine" (p. 28).

In almost all my interviews with new presidents, variations on this theme were reported. One president said:

> The best I can do is sixteen to eighteen hours a day—I'm fifty-one years old! I cannot spend enough time on the urgent things that must be done. There simply is not enough time, and that is the frustration.

One chancellor reported a schedule that included appointments every half-hour from 8:00 A.M. to 5:00 P.M. Mail was taken home and read with dinner, after which the chancellor returned to the office to dictate and handle the paper work. The new chancellor felt it necessary to accede to every request for an appointment, and the staff contributed to this overloading.

Unless a president determines to control his or her own schedule and calendar, there is a presumption that all blank spaces on that calendar are available to be filled in. I have even seen president's secretaries reveal the president's schedule and open times to callers seeking an appointment, with little or no attempt to screen the purpose of the appointment or attempt to refer the caller to someone who might, more directly, deal with the purpose of the call.

My experience has been to postpone work on a budget hearing, a grant proposal, an important speech, or planning document because my days were filled with appointments to see people who thought it necessary to see me. It took a while for me to realize that budgeting and speaking were tasks which I had to perform that also had a claim on my time and schedule. Not all such tasks could be squeezed in before bedtime or before breakfast. One new president, reflecting on this problem, said:

> One must learn to schedule things that often go unscheduled. You need to schedule time to write a speech, time to think and time to deal with correspondence. The president must schedule himself to deal with crucial

long-range problems as well as responding to today's issues and problems. You have to have the right kind of person doing the scheduling for you and changing the expectations of people who want to see you.

Exhaustion and finding time for one's own agenda and one's family were referred to frequently in my discussions with new presidents. In fact, these problems were the main reference point when they speculated about how long they might stay in their new positions.

Leadership Expectations

The president as heroic leader is the image that dominated in the past. I have seen a few cases where the president of a small, independent college stood between the continuance or the bankruptcy and closure of the college, but these have been rare indeed. More typically, the new presidents find the constraints on leadership and influence so great that they soon disparage the "heroic" notion. One public college president completing a difficult first year scoffed at my question about leadership with the remark, "I have to laugh when people talk about the power of a president."

In the larger institutions, presidents and chancellors learned to scale down their expectations about power and influence. Where there is a mature form of faculty governance, and decision making is decentralized, through committees and departments, the new president must refrain from proposing a solution or new program and having all the duly constituted committees sit in judgment on the merits of the idea. Rather, the president has to pose the problem in such a way that he or she can judge the proposals that come to the president for approval.

Eric Ashby, writing of administrators in British universities, describes how administrators must conceal their bright ideas.

> In British universities naked enterprise on the part of a university president is regarded with suspicion, not to say alarm. If a British university president has a bright idea (and he does have bright ideas in his early years of office), it would be the height of ineptitude to publish it to his faculty, and fatal to issue a directive about it. He must unobtrusively—if possible anonymously—feed it into the organization at a low level, informally over lunch, and watch it percolate slowly upwards. With luck it will come back on to his desk months later for approval, and he must greet it with the pleased surprise parents exhibit when their children show them what Santa Claus has brought them for Christmas. To do this over some reform urgently needed in the oganization requires a singular degree of equanimity; but the university president who is not prepared to discipline his initiative in this way fails (pp. 99–100).

My own impression is that a new president tends to overestimate the influence he or she will have and by the end of the first year, presidents tend to exaggerate their lack of influence. The fact is that as the president is seen as effective, with the governing board, or legislature, or in fund-raising, or with the faculty, the president's influence increases. If the growing influence is accompanied by his or her taking strong stands on matters of importance and principle, the leadership influence grows. Taking strong stands may require a display of willingness to lay one's job on the line, which is only a source of strength if it is clear that it is seriously meant and not a kind of petulance. Failure to use influence on important matters becomes a sign of weakness and has its costs. It is a delicate balance.

Cohen and March (p. 120) refer to the "power-expectation gap" in describing a similar dynamic at work. They say that "presidents should ordinarily experience systematic increases in the complaints about their timidity over time and systematic decreases in the complaints about their illegitimacy."

There are many areas in which new presidents have a great deal of influence and in which they may take initiatives. These include setting budget priorities, controlling some areas of personnel selection, long-range planning, physical plant, and program development. It is in the core academic areas where the constraints on a new president's influence are greatest. One new president of a major independent university said to me, "I could get a new school or college created here without much trouble, but it would be difficult for me to influence the curriculum or even the quality of faculty for it."

My experience reinforces the finding that a president's least amount of influence is in the area of what takes place in the classrooms, labora-tories, and libraries of a college or university. The student-teacher trans-actions are not controlled by the president. Only through persuasion, encouragement, creation of an environment, the honoring and rewarding of important values does the president influence the learning experience and outcomes.

Coping with External Forces

Almost without exception, the discrepancies between expectations and realities concerning off-campus constraints occurred in the public insti-tutions and especially in multicampus systems. Although presidents of independent colleges have many challenges and problems, they have a sense of personal freedom to act which is missing in the public sector. (I will describe the problems within systems in chapter six.)

Those presidents who had moved from the private sector to a public institution were especially surprised by the unexpected involvements with governmental entities. Even those presidents who had gone from lower positions in public institutions were startled by the extent of contacts with state government. One tends to be aware of the need to maintain communication with the governor and to prepare a sound case for one's budget request to the legislature. What is surprising is the day-to-day dealings with a variety of state agencies affecting personnel, purchasing, building, travel, collective bargaining, auditing, and the like. Further, conferring with the legislature does not occur only once a year, which fact mildly irritated some new presidents while others threatened to resign if it got no better.

One new president, commenting on the governance arrangement in his state and the political aspects of the system, said, "If I had known what I was getting into regarding the state bureaucracy and the red tape of working in this system, I would never have taken this presidency."

The frustration of trying to understand how and by whom political decisions get made is obviously a challenge to a new public university president. One such president has been in correspondence with me about the "elusive character" of state political power and decision making:

> For a president to be effective, he has to address those decision-making processes in ways which will be heard and will influence the outcome. Even with very capable legislative liaison people, the actual access to the decision-making process becomes difficult and the realities of the situation elusive. I have found myself wanting to act in a decisive way, to speak so that the needs of the institution might be heard and understood, to be effective where it counted. I am not at all sure that, after two years, I have any understanding of the processes, or the people, or where the power to decide really rests.

In some states, politics intrudes on everything. A new state college president in an eastern state described how a recently completed building had taken eight years of planning and five years for construction, with high costs and inferior quality. Patronage expectations also were shocking to him and he was given a difficult time by two legislators at a public budget hearing, because, someone conjectured, he failed to comply with their patronage requests.

In this same eastern state, I heard several ironic remarks about affirmative action requirements. It seems that the new regulations were becoming an effective weapon against patronage pressures from legislators. One president told me that his stock answer to such pressure was that all hiring was now done after a search under affirmative action, and he could not control the hiring process. That seemed to satisfy some people.

It is frustrating to be held accountable for an institution and yet to have so many constraints on one's exercise of authority and responsibility. The perception of those constraints, often anonymous in nature, is an unpleasant surprise to many new presidents. For the most part governing boards seem oblivious to these constraints and, in some cases, aid and abet their continuation by their own links to the state officials.

I have tried to identify and explain those first-year experiences that stand out in the minds of presidents completing their first year of service. I have restricted myself to a selected listing of functional areas; it by no means includes all the areas identified as having discrepancies between expectations and realities. Also omitted is the area of the personal side of the new presidential experience, which obviously has functional ramifications. That area will be described in chapter eight.

5/ The President and the Governing Board

Nothing is more important to a college or university president than a successful relationship with that institution's governing board. It is the governing board that determines or arranges for the forms of institutional governance. It is the governing board that delegates authority to the president. Without a sound relationship with the governing board, the president cannot be effective.

The Association of Governing Boards has developed Self-Study Guidelines and Criteria to assist boards of various kinds of institutions in assessing the effectiveness of their own performance. Among the eleven criteria identified for self-assessment is criterion 7, "Board/Chief Executive Relations," as follows:

> Trustees and the chief executive officer share at least one major
> characteristic: they have a total institutional perspective. The quality of
> the "working relationship" between the board and the executive officer
> is of critical importance to the effectiveness of each. While the board
> must take responsibility for basic policies and their consequences it must
> also give the chief executive the authority and flexibility to act decisively.

It has been stated that the president serves "at the pleasure of the board." How does a board determine its own role, responsibility, and authority—which make up its perspective—so that it can determine its pleasure or displeasure with its chief executive officer, the president? How does it come to be that the highest institutional authority consists of a group of part-time, unpaid trustees—men and women who are often far removed from the day-to-day activities of a college or university?

It is not my intention to present a history of governing boards or governance in this essay, but it is important to understand some basic facts. The practice of governance by lay boards of citizens is a very special characteristic of American colleges and universities which needs to be understood if we are to have any perspective on their interrelationship with presidents, faculties, or students.

Origins of the Governing Board

Originating in the medieval church, universities and colleges were monitored and, if necessary, controlled by the agent of the church, called chancellor. There was no external secular control over such schools. The internal leaders were elected by representatives of the faculty or students. Later, by the fourteenth and fifteenth centuries, the church-appointed chancellor had become largely a figurehead. However, as state authority replaced church authority, the central government exercised the external control. "Independent" universities were not a part of the continental experience.

Beginning with the establishment of the colonial colleges, American institutions were independent of a central government. Instead, they utilized the concept of a lay board or independent board of trustees in governance. This approach was consistent with the pattern of lay boards for Protestant churches and, in fact, was a pattern also being developed in Holland for its universities.

At the close of the colonial period, all nine American colleges were governed by lay boards, to whom the college charters had been given. Since the United States Constitution left the matter of education to the individual states, it seemed natural for those states to continue the practice of granting charters to boards of trustees for new institutions and to create similar boards of trustees when establishing state colleges or universities. For public institutions, the statutes, or constitutional provisions, specified the methods by which such trustees would be appointed or elected and, unlike the independent college, such boards were not self-perpetuating.

What is unusual about American public higher education, therefore, is that the lay board of control is the accepted form for governing our diverse institutions and such a form is meant to keep them relatively independent from *direct* state or governmental dictation.

The Trustee Role

The concept of a "trustee" is relatively easy to understand, especially in the context of an independent institution. The trustee "holds in trust" the assets of an estate, utilizing them in the manner intended by expressed provisions of that estate. Similarly, the creation of an educational institution expresses purposes and values to be transmitted and preserved. Both the property or fiscal assets and such purposes and values are entrusted to the board of trustees. Thus, they have the supreme legal responsibility for both fiscal and policy matters. How to exercise that authority, what to delegate to the president or faculty, when to intervene into management and administrative matters—these are perennial questions not easily answered except as they are raised.

Based on the traditions of independent colleges and the concept of trusteeship, governing boards may be expected to be champions of the institutions they serve in this unique capacity. At the same time, those people who hold such expectations of governing boards may also resent trustee questioning of operations or faculty activities.

For the public institution or system of institutions, the trustee role may be difficult to describe. Certainly the faculty expectation of advocate must be matched to the legislator's expectation of watchdog, defender of the public interest, or perhaps investigator. Yet there are important instances of public university governing boards standing up to state government pressures or threats and resisting improper demands. Perhaps the greatest distortion of the trustee model is in the single boards of multi-institutional systems. In such cases, the board may assume an arms-length relationship with its individual institutions, in order to act as guardian or "trustee" for the public.

Within this context of vague and conflicting role expectations, I want to discuss the working relationships of a president and governing board.

There are a variety of descriptions concerning the major responsibilities of governing boards. Nason (1974) reviews and summarizes much of this literature. The Association of Governing Boards publishes several pamphlets concerning trustee responsibilities. The Carnegie Commission on Higher Education (1973) describes the functions governing boards should serve. Yet a good deal of ambiguity remains when it comes to applying such formulations.

Many humorous anecdotes, usually attributed to presidents, describe the duties of the governing board. Essentially, these anecdotes revolve around the theme of inaction; that is, the governing board should meet to appoint the new president, then adjourn until such time as they want to fire the president. The meaning is clear—presidents resent having board members questioning their actions or telling them how to perform their tasks.

Greenleaf (1977) in a remarkably provocative book that I commend to presidents and trustees discusses what he considers to be a "conceptual flaw" in the way our institutions are structured. The flaw, as he sees it, is the absence of a provision for trustees to be a functioning part of the institution's leadership. He attributes this flaw largely to the historical role of administrators:

> Administrators have been with us for several millennia, ever since the
> first person undertook to mobilize and direct the energies of other people
> toward a defined goal. Consequently, administration was seen as a wholly

sufficient process long before there were trustees. The original administrators may have been the arm of despotic power, with crude sanctions at their disposal. Later they were circumscribed somewhat by law and custom, whether they were agents of government or of a private employer. Yet much of the notion (established long ago) of absoluteness and self-sufficiency of administrators survives today in the accepted concepts of organization. . . . In the face of historical precedent and practice, it is small wonder that administrators have not accepted trustees as an important influence, and that trustees have not seen fit to establish their appropriate roles (p. 92).

Whatever description of a governing board's responsibilities you may wish to cite, then, the very highest priority is given to the selection of a president, the maintenance of effective relations with that president, and the responsibility for replacing that president when the board is no longer pleased. Being part-time, unpaid volunteers, individual trustees may not feel the import of this priority particularly. To the president, however, at the apex of a professional career, the vulnerability of such a relationship is deeply felt. Board insensitivity to this fact can be very disturbing to a president.

Presidential Authority

I have mentioned the importance of legitimating the authority of the president through the process of presidential selection. The entire issue of authority is vexing in a college or university. Under our system of governance, the state confers a charter upon the trustees of a private or independent college. Their board of trustees becomes, therefore, the supreme legal authority of that institution. Similarly, most state statutes, or state constitutions, vest supreme legal authority in a governing board of a state institution. In the public college or university, then, the board is *both* the highest legal authority within the institution's structure of governance and an agent of the state. Appointments to public boards are achieved through the legal authority of the state. As Perkins notes (1973, p. 207), "The board is both the symbol and the fact of institutional authority."

No matter what the tradition or mythology of a community of scholars may connote, even the awarding of academic degrees is by action of the governing board in American institutions. The faculty *recommends* that appropriate persons receive specific degrees. It is the board's authority to grant or not grant degrees.

The authority of a president, therefore, is the authority that the governing board wishes to delegate to its chief executive officer. Depending upon the institution or system, and its experience, that delegation may be extensive or relatively minor. The extent to which a president is seen as operating within a broad delegation of authority is the extent to which a president is seen as strong in the eyes of the various constituencies.

Whatever authority is delegated to the president is usually constrained by two factors: first, that such authority will be utilized within the policies and guidelines established by the board; and, secondly, that the more significant actions of the president are subject to the board's review. The authority thus delegated to the president is, quite properly, within the constraints that it be exercised in a duly authorized manner.

I am speaking of legal authority here. Quite obviously, there is also an educational authority that flows from the authoritativeness of scholars and scientists—the faculty. They confer on the president a form of *de facto* educational authority or legitimacy by their consent to have the president represent their interests to the governing board. When they withdraw such consent, it is difficult for the president to assert his or her legitimacy. Despite one's legal authority, it is hard to operate a productive school against the will of those who are its teachers or students. (The problem that faculty collective bargaining presents to the president and governing board will be discussed in chapter seven.)

For the most part, members of governing boards have not served as college presidents. They cannot be expected to understand all of the issues that deserve their attention nor just how much authority to delegate to a president. It is my strong belief that a president must not refrain from playing the role of teacher with a governing board, increasing members' understanding, suggesting proper boundaries between the respective roles, and providing constant feedback to improve the performance of both the board and the president.

Above all, the president and the board must keep in mind that everyone knows what legal authority exists. It is the legitimacy of that authority as it is exercised that becomes the bench mark for resistance or cooperation.

Subject to Review

A strong board ought to want a strong president. A strong president will not attempt to weaken a board's authority. On the contrary, the authority of a president is enhanced by a board that insists on the need to approve major policy and fiscal matters, including the awarding of tenure, and exercises the right to review all decision making by the president. Although on its face this stand by the board may seem to reflect weakness in a president, actually it provides needed strength and power. If the board awaits a president's recommendation, and acts to support or even to question that recommendation, it is difficult to make end runs around the president directly to the board. If important decisions are subject to review, the president can utilize such a possibility as a constraint in situations where pressures are great for questionable actions. If everyone knows that the board will have to be provided with evidence and a rationale for any decision, or a specific recommendation from its chief executive officer, it becomes difficult to precipitate unwise actions. Further, it becomes clear to all that the president has to become convinced of the merits of a proposal, since it is the president who will play the crucial role of presenting and recommending any actions on matters before the board.

I believe that when a board is determined to be accountable, the president's role is strengthened. It becomes crucial to any major action.

One illustration of this point comes from the late 1960s, when militant student protest often resulted in various "demands" for institutional policy changes. Weak boards, particularly evident in the private sector, were sometimes run over by the capitulation of faculty councils or presidents to the rage of the moment. A strong board, however, which required appropriate review, hearings, evidence, and a consideration of the long-range public interest, helped in resisting unwarranted pressures. I believe a strong president wants a strong board as a court of last resort.

Even in academic and faculty personnel matters, my premise is still valid, I believe. Academic units should be aware that the board has a systematic plan for program review, which requires evidence of quality, need, and the like. This policy provides the basis for the president's monitoring of quality. Likewise, the possibility of having to defend a tenure recommendation, on its merits, is a necessary restraint against lowering faculty performance standards.

The spirit in which the board exercises its right of review is, of course, crucial to its effectiveness. If the president is seen as unable to get the board to act in a rational, predictable manner, then the process becomes counterproductive. The board shapes the institution in many important ways by helping the president understand what the board will or will not approve and thus influencing the decisions the president will make. The president then becomes the key to the decision-making process and will be blamed if the process is dysfunctional. The board's work becomes impossible without an effective president as its chief executive officer.

Expectations

I have discussed role expectations in connection with new college presidents. This same concept is useful in understanding some of the conflict between presidents and boards over expectations that may not be reasonable.

The president may make certain assumptions about the desire of the board to be advocates of the institution and may be disappointed with the lack of support for a request for a significant increase in appropriations. Or the president may expect automatic respect from the board for a carefully considered faculty senate recommendation, only to find that key members discount faculty views and regard faculty as unproductive slackers concerned only with their own self-interest. Presidents often find that individual board members have expectations that are difficult to live with.

For example, some board members have political or legislative experiences and may assume that they have power and authority to act as individuals. They may seek to have influence, as individuals, making strong "suggestions" to the president rather than putting forth their proposals for board vote. The expectation that the president should try to keep each board member satisfied is an impossible one for a president.

Similarly, some board members only have experience with a business organization and make the analogy of the president as manager. They assume that when the owner of the business makes a policy, the manager should implement it or be discharged. Trustees who fail to understand that a president must also take into account the expectations and traditions of the faculty, staff, and students and cannot merely carry out "orders" often are angered, feeling that a president is thwarting the will of the board.

The president has a vital political role. It is not a sign of weakness for the president to be seen as concerned with the interests of all constituent groups and not only the governing board. Rather, it is a sign of strength that helps the president to be effective in guiding the board in its policy-making work, as well as implementing their policy decisions.

Expectations should be explicit and constantly reviewed by both boards and their presidents. These should be clarified at the time of a presidential appointment and revisited at least annually when reviewing the performance of the president. Above all, they should not remain a mystery.

The president is employed by the governing board, but should be regarded as a knowledgeable partner in leading the enterprise, not as a subservient employee of the board. The expectation of leadership is crucial to the role. When it is not forthcoming, the board should express its displeasure.

Communication between Board and President

Candor is essential in the relationship between an institution's board and the president. In many ways, the quality of that relationship is on display each time the board meets. The quality becomes obvious to interested constituents and the public, not only in the actual decisions made or approved by the board but also in the nature of the interchanges and communication. For the independent college or university, such exchanges may be quite private and confidential. For the public institution, such exchanges are far more frequent and almost always public. The special problem of communication between board and president of public institutions deserves attention.

In the past decade many states have enacted, or strengthened existing, legislation concerning meetings of public bodies. Generally, such statutes include provisions related to due notice to the public of all meetings and agenda; that such meetings be open to the public; some manner in which the public may make its views known about the agenda issues; and some description of the requirements for making the records of meetings available to the public. The laws are referred to as open-meeting or sunshine laws.

Kaplowitz (1978) has described the impact of such laws on governing boards of public colleges and universities. Of major concern here is the effect of such laws on president/governing board communication. Two key questions arise within the bounds of each state's legislation: what constitutes a meeting, and what topics, if any, justify going into executive session that is not open to the public. In some states, a "meeting" may be said to occur and fall within the provisions of a statute when two or more members of a board or committee come together and discuss any matter of public business. Premeeting dinners, social hours, retreats, and the like become prohibited under the law unless the "public" is able to attend as well. In practice, public in this context means the press.

Under some states' statutes, executive session is permitted for personnel issues. In other states, such is not possible. Florida and Minnesota laws require that even the names of persons being considered for the presidency of a state university are a matter of public record.

Clearly, then, the functioning of a board, and manner of communication of a president with that board, are severely affected by open-meeting laws. The cohesiveness of a board is made more difficult by the absence of informal interactions such as those that occur at social occasions. But, most serious is the constraint on the president of sharing informally with the board the airing of sensitive issues, long-range concerns, and even the tensions that might exist between certain board members and the president. Executive sessions in which the board and the president, and perhaps senior staff, express themselves candidly about their problems have become a thing of the past in many states. In their place are often stilted discussions at open meetings, during which the president may hint about an impending problem and back off of a pointed question as the news reporter present raises pencil to pad. Board members may feel inhibited about disagreeing with a president, or questioning sharply, assuming that such behavior will be interpreted as a lack of confidence in the president. If significant sharing of information and concerns is only possible in a clandestine manner, the public interest is not being served. If fundamental disagreement can only be expressed as a matter of public record, no institution is well served. We can and have adjusted to the new "morality," but something of great value has been lost, in my opinion.

Care and Feeding of Board Members

Anyone who has been a college or university president has experienced the problem of trying to respond to the needs or desires of individual board members. While such interactions may have a pleasant side, they are often a source of irritation and are very time-consuming.

Depending upon the kind of institution one is identifying, the illustrations will differ. Some circumstances are common, however. Should individual board members, or their important friends, be put up at the president's house when they are in town? If so, is the president's spouse expected to be available as housekeeper, cook, and charming entertainer? Is a request or suggestion from a board member expected to be acted upon as a command? For example, does a trustee's invitation to a private social event represent a command performance in which the president's appearance is more than a casual expectation? Getting good tickets to football games, being properly seated (protocol considerations) at various campus events, being included or excluded at other events, all concern some board members and impact on presidents. Some board members exploit their appointment by trying to involve the president or his staff in social contacts with their personal friends and even their business clients.

Another aspect of the care-and-feeding issue relates directly to board and institution matters. Some board members attempt to get a president committed in a partisan issue that is to come before the board, such as committee chairmanships, and the like. If a president listens to the complaint of one board member about another, without comment, it may be construed as agreement. There may be disappointment if a president fails to "take sides" when a disagreement occurs between such board members.

Perhaps the most difficult expectations a president has to deal with come from those board members who, by virtue of their occupations or positions, may expect special and personal briefings on all matters pertaining to their interests. An example is the physician or dentist trustee who insists on being consulted before any action is taken on all health-related programs. Such persons may try to dominate decision making about such program areas, even judging faculty and dean recommendations, not as board members, but as superior professionals. Board members who are professionals in law, business, athletics, the arts, or other areas may display similar attitudes. This phenomenon places a burden on the president to spend considerable time with individual board members. Perhaps a more serious problem is the abdication by other board members of their responsibility, as members of a corporate body, to exercise their collective judgment in all matters requiring board action.

Improving the President/Board Relationship

I have attempted to identify the problems and factors that lead to difficulty in the working relationships of presidents and boards. Quite clearly, though, there are many situations in which the board is delighted with its president and is content to follow his or her lead in most matters. I find that such contentment nearly always occurs in those independent institutions where the president has been successful in fund raising and maintaining a balanced budget. In the marginal institution, struggling to remain solvent, the president is often the "scapegoat" for all constituencies, including the governing board. Somewhere in between is the public institution president, where political skills may be more crucial to success than anything else. Here the delicate balancing act—not only with the faculty, staff, students, and alumni, but also among the governing board members—is an exhausting test of one's endurance and survival skills.

Can a president identify any actions or behaviors that might improve his or her chance for success in balancing the various forces? I suggest some items for consideration.

1. There should be regular efforts made to clarify the mutual expectations of both boards and presidents. At the very least, there should be the opportunity to revisit priorities of effort and policy planning annually. Such an opportunity should enable the president to express concerns about board behavior as well as the board expressing its expectations of the president. The board's failure to clarify its concerns can only confuse the president and distract him or her from effective functioning.

2. The president must be educator and teacher to the institution's various publics, but especially the board. Unless a board is confident that the president is informing them of the significant issues confronting the institution, enlightened board members will seek such information elsewhere. A measure of the president's leadership ability will be the board's active concern with the vital issues facing the institution and its well-being.

3. A president should avoid any private or personal agreements with individual board members. The president should be free at all times to take a position based on his or her best judgment and not modified by prior commitments that cater to the personal interest of a board member. Similarly, board members should avoid personalizing their concerns and acting as though a president's refusal to support a pet idea is a repudiation

of their own worth. The essential purposes and value of the institution to society should be the bench mark against which all matters are decided.

4.   The board itself should take some responsibility for improving its effectiveness through new appointments. Thus, in the public institutions, boards would find ways to convey to governors the needs for strong, dedicated, nonpartisan appointees. In independent institutions, criteria would be established to assess board performance and needs. Future appointments to the board would be based upon such an assessment and new members would be fully aware of expectations held for their performance and contributions.

5.   Boards should assume that problems and conflicts are part of the normal day-to-day functioning of any institution. They should not react overly to "bad" news that the press or other media may choose to publicize. We should have long ago overcome our fantasies of campuses as Gardens of Eden and the innocence that accompanies such images. Institutions are communities and, especially with limitations on resources, they are communities in conflict. Appropriate procedures and processes for dealing with that conflict, and leadership that does not allow that conflict to become a substitute for purpose, are what boards must insist upon. They cannot insist on the absence of conflict.

6.   Finally, the board must assume responsibility for the working conditions of its president. No one else will be able to respond to a president's need for staff, adequate housing conditions, health, encouragement, or uplifted morale. If the board does not care about the welfare of its president, it will get what it probably deserves—a president who doubts the value of expending himself or herself on behalf of the board and its institution.

In chapter six, I will discuss special concerns that relate to presidents in multicampus institutions and the requirement that they deal with governing boards through a system executive officer.

6/ Presidents and Chancellors in Multicampus Systems

One development in public higher education deserves special attention. The growth of systems of colleges and universities, under single governing boards, has accelerated greatly in the past two decades. Lee and Bowen (1971) used one definition of system but there are many other ways to identify systems of institutions. My concern here is multiple campuses, or institutions, that operate under a single board that employs a chief executive officer of the system (titled president or chancellor); each campus or institution in the system is headed, in turn, by a chief executive officer (titled chancellor or president). Thus, there is a separate system office, with its professional staff, and institutional staffs operating each institution. This arrangement appears to be the trend in public post-secondary education, for reasons I shall describe.

The problems of systems that deserve attention, and often do not get it, stem from three key role conflict situations: (1) governing board—head of system relationships; (2) system head—campus president relationships; and (3) governing board—campus president relationships. In this discussion, a *president* is the system chief executive officer and a *chancellor* is the campus chief executive officer. I know that these titles develop out of historical accident, rather than a rational taxonomy. They might be reversed in some states. Thus, in the University of Wisconsin System, the University of California System, and the University of North Carolina System, the title of *president* is used for the head of the system. However, the State University of New York (SUNY), the California State University and Colleges system, and the State University System of Minnesota use the title of *chancellor* for the head of the system.

There are many explanations for the development of multicampus systems of higher education. In some cases, such systems resulted from the creation of branch campuses in the late 1940s and early 1950s as enrollment burgeoned and students could not be accommodated in the one central campus of a state institution. In some cases, systems were planned originally, as with some community colleges that were launched as systems to meet the needs of a metropolitan region. Some states had single governing boards for their teachers' colleges and as these institutions developed into comprehensive institutions, the single board with a central office remained at the top. In the 1960s, however, state officials became increasingly concerned with accountability, wasteful competition, and unnecessary duplication and with improved planning, coordination, and management. From these concerns came demands for getting control over a variety of forces, seemingly out of control, that were exerting increasing claims on public revenues.

In many cases, consolidations and systems were created by elected officials who were subjected to great political pressures by board members and constituents of single state institutions in a vigorous competition with other institutions. Governors and legislators might be forced to choose between institutions or give everyone what they wanted to avoid conflict. Priorities were being set by political decisions in the appropriation process, rather than through coordinated planning at the state level. In some states, powerful coordinating boards were created to review budget and program requests from the various systems of institutions that had developed. Illinois, for example, has five separate systems of postsecondary institutions, plus a statewide board of higher education for budget review and planning purposes. In other states, such as Florida, all nine state universities were placed under one governing board of nine members, with a system office headed by a chancellor. In Wisconsin, all twenty-seven campus units of the University of Wisconsin and State Universities of Wisconsin were merged into a single system, with a single governing board and central administration headed by a president. Each state has dealt with such consolidations somewhat differently but the impact is similar. In many public institutions today, there is a new layer of administration between the chief campus executive officer and the governing board. There is growing centralization of authority and decision making. This trend affects faculty governance on the campus level and many system administrators have seen the election of collective bargaining by the faculty as a result. Faculty organization further justifies centralization and strengthens the need for a system office and staff, in addition to strengthening the role of state officials in higher education governance. The greater involvement of the state in higher education, in turn, increases systemization and bureaucratization of decision making, altering the role of the campus administrator and making it seem less personally significant and rewarding. Let me examine the import of this chain of consequences.

Single Governing Board of a System

As we have seen in chapter 5, the concept of "trusteeship" of the independent, church-related college was adapted for the public institution as the form of governing our colleges and universities. Since board members of public institutions were appointed by political leaders, as guardians of the public interest, as well as advocates of institutions, the trusteeship model was somewhat distorted. With the advent of single governing boards for systems of institutions, the model is strained beyond recognition. Yet we have no other model, except that of direct control of state agencies by the executive branch of government, with oversight from the legislature. Accordingly, system presidents are coming to be seen as responsive to governors and legislatures. Their role, too, is increasingly ambiguous as pressures mount.

Campus heads, whom I shall call chancellors here, have expectations of governing boards that flow from the original trusteeship model. Thus, they expect that board members will have an interest in their problems and their campus, be familiar with its leaders, and visit it from time to time, attending important events. More often than not, they are doomed to disappointment. One campus chancellor, reflecting on his first year in a ten-campus system, said to me,

> When the board hired me I told them of my strong desire for the trustees
> to visit the campus and get acquainted with our faculty and students.
> They said they would, but so far I have only had one trustee come to the
> campus the whole year, although I have invited them on at least fifteen
> occasions. In the selection process they said they would come. Other
> than my own personal hurt, I think it is very bad professionally.

More and more, system governing boards are unable to be aware of campus activities or the feelings of students and faculty. They are only made aware of crises. They insert the system president and staff between themselves and campus staff. Campus chancellors report to the system president. Instead of filling the buffer role of trustees, system boards become concerned with coordination, assignment of eagerly sought new programs, eliminating duplication, resource reallocation, and investigation of complaints from various segments of state government and the public.

I do not ascribe any malevolence to any of this failure of system boards to focus on individual campuses. The role of single governing boards becomes more and more difficult as administrative layers pile up. In some systems, each campus may also have an advisory board or local board of trustees, which campus chancellors often regard as ineffectual or worse. One campus chancellor in North Carolina, where each campus does have a local board of trustees under the systemwide board of governors, disabused me of the thought that there is value in campus boards in a system. He noted, "It's very difficult to find things for the board of trustees to do since the board of governors has all the power." He was required to dream up an agenda for local trustee meetings and otherwise keep his local board happy, in addition to working with the system office and board. Dealing with the local board became an additional burden.

In light of this increasingly common form of organization in the public sector, let us examine the role of system president, before looking further at the experiences of campus chancellors.

System Presidents

Although it is difficult to generalize about any leadership role in the diverse systems of higher education, it seems clear that the system presidency is the least stable and often the least personally satisfying. The turnover rate in system presidencies also seems to be somewhat higher than that of campus chancellors. Obviously, system presidents get caught between the ambiguous expectations of single boards and the tendency of the respective campuses to blame all ills on the system administration.

The role of system president is relatively new and there is no tradition to guide one's expectations. Thus, expectations of performance differ and are highly contradictory. Some board members might anticipate that a system president will bring the campus chancellors into line, to take command, and run the system. Others may see the system president as merely a coordinator, not a manager, giving greatest priority to being an effective spokesperson and representative of the system with the legislature and the public. The expectations of the governor and legislature may be in conflict with board expectations. Most often, they want greater control at the top of the system.

On several occasions I have tried to discern the rationale and purpose of a system, with consequent role definition for its president, from relevant board meeting minutes or the legislative history, but these sources have not helped. The legislation for the creation of a single university system in Wisconsin does contain language that may be of some guidance. It speaks of a system of institutions and the text describing the responsibilities of the board of regents includes ". . . promote the widest degree of institutional autonomy within the controlling limits of systemwide policies and priorities established by the board." Nevertheless, new legislators, governors, and regents interpret this in the light of changing contexts. It seems that everything is "subject to" something else.

The role of the system president, then, will most often be shaped by the early incumbents, rather than by written definitions. It is a role that develops out of actions taken on a case-by-case basis, becoming precedents for future actions. The style and experience of the first system president may play a large part in shaping the nature of the system office. Thus, a veteran campus chancellor, trusted by many in the system, may become the system president and decentralize almost all operations except for a budget planning and management information system. A council of campus chancellors might be formed to advise the system president and have a major decision-making role, including veto power. At the other extreme, a first system president may be hired from industry or the military, with no campus administrative experience. Such a person might move to centralize all operations and decision making, developing manuals and directives for all possible contingencies, processes, and procedures.

The system president will interact directly with the governing board and may choose to present all agenda items without the participation of the campus chancellors. Others will insist that the interpretation and explanation of an agenda item pertaining to a campus be made by the campus chancellor. The status of the campus chancellor, in the eyes of the board and the campus constituencies, is severely affected by the manner in which the system president calls on campus chancellors for their counsel.

As leader and spokesperson, some system presidents attempt to know about everything within the entire system—daring to respond to any and every question raised by the press or legislature. Such a style obviously requires one to get detailed information about all matters and hold campus executives at arms-length in public. The opposite style is to display one's general knowledge of the overall value and activity of the system but to defer to appropriate campus officers for their responses to questions requiring detailed knowledge of specific campus matters. The latter style obviously communicates the importance of campus officials.

In relations with the legislature, a system head may be seen as effective politically, while guarding the governance processes of the campuses and their faculty participation in decision making. Other system presidents may appear to have established efficacious relationships with the legislature at the expense of giving away highly prized campus governance prerogatives.

One can explicate these dichotomies of style further, but the point has been made. There is often a vacuum to be filled when a system is created and the personal style and previous experience of the early incumbents will play a major part in shaping the role expectations of system presidents.

System Administration Staff

A system central office and staff can become a convenient foil for campus malcontent. "Blame it on the system" can become a cliché resorted to by those who are keenly aware of antibureaucratic prejudices. System staff can get caught in the middle, and, thus, it is important to analyze their place in this picture of organizational complexity.

It is useful to look, again, at two extremes of system organization and function. A system office and staff may be established to function as superordinates of campus staff, pre-auditing, controlling, and supervising operations. In such a case, campus counterpart staff are not certain whether their loyalties are to their campus chancellor or to the system office. In the opposite model, the system office staff are seen as resource persons/consultants, available to aid campuses with expertise not readily available and to run interference for the campuses with the state agencies and legislative staff. These illustrations are extremes, but the direction of any system office is clearly toward one pole or the other.

Two illustrations of the effect of each model on functional areas may further illuminate this topic. In the first illustration, some state systems centralize all contacts with state government so that these provide consistent and accurate information to important questions. Nevertheless, campus chancellors and their staffs are not sure the questions are being answered correctly and are suspicious that system staff identify themselves as being more in league with their counterparts in state government than with those on the campuses. Instead of being a buffer, system staff are often seen as having lowered the last barriers to direct state interference by their inept dealing with state government officials.

The second and related illustration flows from the need of the system office to provide information to various state agencies and the legislature. An overly zealous system staff, eager to respond to any and all requests for data from state officials, may establish a management information system that makes enormous demands on the campuses and seems to serve no functional campus needs. Having to feed that management system from each campus, without any appreciation of its relevance, can generate in local staff a great discontent and suspicion. This outcome is especially true when the information is kept at the system office and not shared with the campus units.

Where faculty have resorted to collective bargaining in a system, negotiations are usually conducted systemwide. Again, this places serious responsibilities in the hands of system staff, with campus chancellors and deans often uninvolved until after the settlements have been made.

A pointed description of how circular and reinforcing the system–campus relationships can be, is written by Leo F. Redfern (1979), who is specifically referring to the Florida University System:

> In theory a strong governing board would be of value in helping system campuses contend with the extensive bureaucracies of state government, such as departments of administration. Because it institutes its own

rules, procedures, and audits, it would seem a system could readily persuade legislatures that good supervision and coordination is being provided by the system, without the necessity for additional (duplicate) state controls. System staff, normally based in the state capitol, could speak to government counterparts with great technical authority; in such capacity they might thereby save considerable time of campus staff who could then devote more attention to their academic administrative duties.

Yet this does not work that way. There is, for example, a "Clockwork Orange" element in the Florida system (which may be typical of many systems nationwide, in this respect): The executive branch agencies, as budget bureaus or departments of administration, are given extensive controls over other state agencies, including the system. To effectuate this responsibility, the control agencies demand more and more explanations about an ever-increasing number of matters. This is countered by a growth in system staff to enable it to respond to such demands. Whereupon the legislature, feeling naturally overwhelmed by all the staff experts in the executive branch, begins to develop its own legislative staff experts who commence, in turn, to ask questions (e.g., "Why does the University of Florida charge a $5 parking fee while Florida International University does not charge parking fees?"). Thus the stage is set for the need to add further system staff to collect information, most of which is not central to education, from the campuses.

Such a condition led the first Florida chancellor to seek greater uniformity and more standardization in the system, in order to be able to respond promptly to any possible array of questions and inquiries. This led, it is claimed, to the appointment of 20 management information system experts. These now continue to develop more elaborate and sophisticated MIS techniques to the point where a great many campus administrators no longer regard the extensive system MIS as relevant or useful to the needs of operating the campuses.

Thus we see a response that has been so typical in the growth of the federal bureaucracy: to solve problems you must spend money and add staff. The last thirty years' experience should be evidence that this approach appears, at best, a palliative. More and more time and treasure go into overhead, and less and less (proportionately) into the desired end product. As a result, while the cost of public higher education continues to climb higher, fewer of the additional dollars go to instructing and educating students or for programs of educational service.

Systems could, it is clear, be of greater help to campuses in relieving them of the burdensome and unproductive parts of state control agencies' rules and procedures. But except for minor instances, system staffs appear either unable to effectuate any streamlining in these areas, or they actually perceive more mutual interests and objectives with state control agencies' staffs than they do with the campus staffs they supervise. This area, of mitigating state control agencies' effects and powers over the campuses, is one where systems could gain a great deal of campus support and appreciation if they would take an aggressive lead in working toward this goal. To this point in time, it remains one where central system staffs have expressed very little commitment or interest (pp. 199–201).

Perhaps most important of all is the concern at the campus level with the qualifications and knowledge of system office staff. Even when the system president is from the academic world, very often system office staff are seen as narrow specialists with no understanding of what it is like to operate a campus. Some system office staff are persons who could not obtain a senior campus post, yet are placed in positions of seeming authority over campus officers. As one campus chancellor in a large system said to me, "The system office tends to be made up of people who do not understand university governance and administration. By and large, they are people who could not make it on a campus! Ideally, system office staff should be able to be regarded as peers by campus chancellors and vice-chancellors."

A wide variety of legitimate concerns exists about the size, authority, role, and management style of the system office and its staff. Most people, including the central governing board members, may be oblivious to the dynamics that flow from these concerns. The campus chancellor, however, feels the impact of the system more than anyone else in higher education.

Students

One further item needs to be mentioned regarding the roles of various constituents and entities in the governance of a higher education system—that of students. Generally, most students on a campus have little or no concern with the impact of a system and its centralized authority. While faculty may decide to deal with the system through collective bargaining, the individual student does not really experience any difference between a single institution or that of a campus in a system.

Student political leaders, however, seem to thrive on the creation of systems and the accompanying centralization. Campus decisions can be appealed to system office staff, who can also be cultivated, sometimes more easily than campus staff. State- or systemwide student government associations can deal with the central board effectively, often getting items of interest to them on the agenda for each meeting and having students placed on various board committees, if not on the board itself. As campus student government wanes, state student associations are formed, and direct lobbying, often with paid staff, commences with the system office, the board, and the legislature. Some of the strongest student lobbies in the country are in states with strong systems: Florida, California, Montana, and New York.

Campus Chancellors in a System

Based on more than forty campus visits and personal interviews with presidents and chancellors over the past three years, I would conclude that campus chief executive officers—or chancellors—in systems have the most complaints about lack of satisfaction in their positions. Most of them have far less authority than they expected to have, despite their seeming responsibilities, and most express discomfort with system governance.

Obviously, some campus chancellors find it helpful to use the antisystem administration bias that exists on campus to avoid difficult problems. Tough issues can be sent "up" to the system office for review, and often delayed for lenghty periods in order for a *system* policy to be devised for such issues. I have heard strong chancellors criticize colleagues they considered weak or passive for requesting a systemwide policy for every controversial matter that arises on their campus, in order to be able to hide behind system policy. One campus chancellor described campus faculty as usually pro-chancellor because "their hostility tends to be focused on central administration and the central board more than on the campus administration. That is sometimes very useful," he said. Yet it is also clear that campus chancellors tend to be judged on the basis of how much they can get out of system administration. It is a double-edged sword.

The leadership expectation of the campus chancellor still remains, regardless of the system. If strong and imaginative leadership at the campus level is still desirable, and I consider that indispensable, we must be mindful of the ways in which the campus chancellor's role may be crippled and trivialized in systems. In some systems, the campus chancellors seem to have been demoted to middle-level managers. They may not speak at board meetings and may not even have any regular meetings with the system president. They may have to rely on second-level system office intermediaries to interpret their needs and concerns.

System presidents must understand the importance of having campus chancellors who are seen as credible leaders and interpreters of campus needs, rather than as middle-management officers sent out from headquarters to do the bidding of the real bosses at system headquarters.

A Closer View

The role of campus chancellor in a system is in need of further study, as is the system president and the central system board. All the traditions and expectations of American higher education, stemming from earlier, single-institution models, need to be adapted creatively to the changes we are experiencing. Significant dangers to higher education I believe are on the horizon. Problems in higher learning institutions lead to greater external demands for sound management and accountability. There seems to be an attitude of *distrust* of our institutions and therefore a requirement for close monitoring of all operations. This requirement increases centralization and centralization increases the need for system and routine in procedures. Rigid procedures eliminate a good deal of the grass roots participation and the responsiveness to local problems, which leads to passivity and griping about bureaucracy and the impossibility of the "system."

The only way to restore the ability of our institutions to be vital and responsive to people's changing needs is to give them more autonomy and hold them accountable for their actions. Instead, we are "freezing" what we now have and do and placing controls over the change process to make it impervious to change. The less we know about what we *ought* to be doing in education, the more we have frozen in place our present practices. There is less and less opportunity for judgment, discretion, or innovation to be permitted, let alone encouraged. It seems to me that when you are in a predicament, you need more—not fewer—degrees of freedom for getting out of that predicament.

A Proper Balance

In order to restore a proper balance between autonomy and control, each multicampus system of institutions must revisit its essential *purpose* as a system. I would challenge anyone to find as that purpose the creation of homogeneity, stultifying creative change, or stifling leadership at the campus level. The justification for a system is planned, purposeful diversity to serve all of the population better, improved planning and coordination, and keeping the state government officials from deciding academic program and educational priorities by making those tough priority decisions *within the system.*

This rationale means that the system president should be a leader and representative of the system and its needs. That person cannot manage or operate all parts of the system. Strong campus chancellors are required to manage such units. Those persons must cooperate with each other and with the system president so that decisions will be made, insofar as it is possible, within the system, and not from without, by state government or other agency representatives.

Relations with state agencies and officials need to be centralized in a system. Requests for data and other information should be answered from a central source and the answers duly authorized for accuracy and consistency. But while campus chancellors should not subvert the authoritativeness of centralized information and responses, the political strength and influence of the local campuses should be drawn upon and utilized for the welfare of the entire system. A "gag" order on campus chancellors dealing with the legislature may be appropriate for some purposes, but it is certainly not appropriate for all purposes.

I readily admit that a proper balance is a delicate balance. But the criteria by which we judge the right and wrong way of achieving the balance should flow naturally from the essential rationale for creating the system in the first place. If there was no rationale, just a political power play, then academic and political leaders should create one that is sensible and functional, enabling the system to make its greatest contribution to the citizenry it serves. The form of organization is a means, not an end in itself. Improving educational services is the goal of the organization. That is the criterion by which system effectiveness is to be measured.

7/ The President and Governance

The mythology, and perhaps the memory, of the North American university goes all the way back to the medieval *universitas* (guild) of the University of Paris. In that model, the masters (faculty) were empowered to decide who was worthy of being a teacher and on what basis students were to be admitted, examined, and graduated. They elected fellow masters to share brief periods of leadership and administrative responsibility.

Yet we know that the beginnings of higher education in America were denominational colleges, in essentially theocratic colonial settlements, with lay governing boards to supervise and, if necessary, police piety, doctrine, and finances. Until well into the late nineteenth century, the direction of our relatively small institutions of higher learning was in the hands of the agent of the governing board, the president. Even the fate and fortune of state institutions were often in the hands of presidents and their vision and political effectiveness were crucial to their institutions.

It was not until the early twentieth century that professors asserted their professional status and won some significant battles over academic freedom. The American Association of University Professors led in this effort, declaring that faculty members were not merely "employees" and that the professorial role required independence and peer judgment in academic decision making. This affirmation was stated not only in terms of self-interest, but also as being essential for the good of society. The basic principles were enunciated in the AAUP "1940 Statement of Principles on Academic Freedom and Tenure."

Rise of Faculty Participation in Governance
The period of vast expansion of higher education, following World War II, has been referred to as the "academic revolution." The professoriate was prized as never before. The demand was unprecedented for their

74

services. The bench mark for success of an administration was its ability to recruit faculty (usually from other institutions) and retain their services by providing the necessary resources and environment. Even governing boards expressed their support of academicians by granting to faculty significant self-governance in academic and faculty personnel matters. Most liberal arts colleges and universities endorsed the 1940 Principles of the AAUP.

The decade of 1955 to 1965 saw the spread of departmental self-governance and virtual autonomy. As the federal government pressed for and rewarded the expansion of graduate study, or merely expansion of enrollments, departments became more able to control their own decisions and budgets. Individual faculty members in many institutions could decide, largely on their own, or with a few colleagues, what they wanted to teach, at what levels, or whether or not to teach or engage in research activities. Decision making was largely in the hands of academic departments, and administrators were expected to *serve* the faculty by implementing faculty decisions, which meant obtaining the necessary facilities and resources. For the most part the administration was expected to facilitate or enable the faculty to "do its thing." At the least, administrators were supposed to keep out of the way.

Herman Wells, who served as president of Indiana University from 1938 to 1962, advised fellow presidents in 1965: "Remind yourself daily that administration must always be the servant, never the master, of the academic community. It is not an end in itself and exists only to further the academic enterprise. It follows, therefore, that the least administration possible is the best" (p. 171).

During this period, the energies of the president were spent primarily on resource acquisition and physical expansion, including establishing branch campuses for many state institutions or systems. The faculties of departments, schools, and colleges within universities took care of their own matters through the medium of faculty self-governance, coordinated by deans. Mostly, inadequate attention was paid to the institution as a whole. Decisions about the *entire* institution were often made by default through the accretion of the decisions made by departments or small groups of self-interested parties. It was the confederation of loosely tied units, often with no common vision or purpose, that led to Clark Kerr's use of the term *multiversity* and his description of the president in the mid-1960s as "mediator."

The process of decision making, and the structures for enabling participation or consultation in that process, are referred to as the *governance* of colleges and universities. Governance tends to reflect the ebb and flow of various historical factors. By the mid-1960s, faculty influence was very strong in universities and liberal arts colleges. Nowhere is this influence better demonstrated than in the 1966 Statement on Government of Colleges and Universities of the AAUP. That statement—a delineation of the principle known as shared authority or shared governance—precedes the advent of collective bargaining. (It is often reported that this statement was approved by the American Council on Education and the Association of Governing Boards. That report is incorrect. The statement was "recognized as significant" and "commended to member institutions and boards" by the ACE and AGB, in 1966. It would be difficult to get agreement on the statement today, in my opinion.)

The 1966 Statement on Government of Colleges and Universities utilizes the organizational concepts developed by Mary Parker Follett. She wrote of the decision-making process and the twin concepts of "communal authority" (the AAUP calls this "joint effort") and "primal authority" (or "primary responsibility" in the AAUP Statement).

The 1966 Statement makes clear that while the governing board operates as the final authority for the institution and the president is the chief executive officer operating under the delegated authority of that board, it is the faculty that have the "primary responsibility for such fundamental areas as curriculum, subject matter and methods of instruction, research, faculty status, and those aspects of student life which relate to the educational process."

Interestingly, the AAUP Statement of 1966 made no attempt to delineate the role of students in governance. It was not until 1970 that a statement of student participation in government of colleges and universities was approved for publication. In that statement students were recognized as a constituency properly participating in joint efforts but restricted their areas of primary responsibility to extracurricular activities and student regulations (not including discipline).

A good deal has changed since the late 1960s. Student protest and disruption have diminished; the public's disenchantment with higher education has lessened. On the increase are demands for accountability and efficiency, the greater utilization of management science concepts and techniques, more centralized control of administration and decision making, as well as retrenchment. The increasing influence of external state and federal controls and requirements places new burdens on governance processes. In light of these shifts, the campus president must cope with antiquated consultative and participatory structures and the expectations those structures still promote. Add to this situation the advent of faculty collective bargaining and the reader can see the press on the president that results. A brief elaboration of these points is found below.

The Vietnam war, preceded by the civil rights movement, brought many challenges to campus authority. While such movements had some faculty sympathizers, it was largely in the area of administrative authority that faculty agreed students should share power. Yet it became apparent that it was faculty power that was seen by militant students as the ultimate foe. Reacting to family pressures to attend college, and ambivalent about sanctuary from the draft such attendance provided, many students resented the necessity of compliance with faculty academic expectations. More and more students came to college without a commitment to those educational values held by the faculty. As expectations grew that colleges and universities possessed the knowledge to solve the problems of peace, urban blight, racial strife, and economic imbalance, so did the discrepancy grow between those expectations and the realities found. As the New Left and the counterculture "desanctified" the knowledge and technology of the university, so too did many in government and industry. Although it was not spoken of too directly, it was obvious by the early 1970s that a public backlash was under way. At the least, there was no automatic allegiance by elected officials to supporting higher education institutions. This erosion of support has been further exacerbated by the so-called glut of Ph.D.'s, reducing faculty mobility, by recession and inflation, and the promise of decline in the population of eighteen year old men and women available to enter our colleges and universities.

Governments and Institutional Governance
With all this change we have witnessed in the past decade a new wave of demands for efficiency and accountability not experienced since the depression of the 1930s. New structures of coordination and control have been created, stimulating the centralization of decision making. At the state level, the executive and legislative branches compete for influence over decision making and priority setting in public institutions. Staff personnel in both branches make demands for information, making centralized Management Information and Reporting Systems a necessity. Statements of goals and objectives, quantitative measures of outcomes, and indices of efficiency are expected in order to demonstrate cost-benefit types of management analyses. These requirements lead to external assessment of faculty activity and productivity with its quantitative proxies of "contact" hours, student credit hours produced, and the like. Faculty are resentful and administrators are blamed for not being effective in stemming the impending tide of such demands.

When the Carnegie Commission on Higher Education issued its final report (1973), they expressed as their single greatest concern regarding governance the growth of state control over colleges and universities. They observed that *"the great change of the past decade was not the*

*vociferous rise of student power but the quiet increase in public power—
by governors, by legislators, by coordinating councils"* (p. 59, emphasis
added).

The federal government has become involved not only in funding
specific college or university programs but also in successfully asserting
that all institutions are "contractors" or "recipients" and must comply
with a wide variety of regulations that affect the entire institution. Such
requirements, including affirmative action efforts, go to the heart of faculty
and departmental prerogatives in recommending who ought to be hired,
promoted, given tenure, or not retained on the faculty. The effect of such
a program as affirmative action is but one example of how the president
can be put in a position that can become uncomfortable as he or she
balances forces exerted by internal constituencies and external authorities.

There is a considerable lag between expectations of the faculty regarding participation in decision making and the new realities that are
affecting presidents and governing boards. All too often, the turnaround
time demanded for compliance with federal rules does not permit adequate
consultation as called for in governance bylaws. Too often, the availability
of resources does not permit more than a decision to *reduce* expenditures
and faculty councils do not like to "approve" such realities. Shared-
authority concepts do not work well when colleagues must determine
which of their number must be eliminated. They would rather blame such
decisions on the "administration." Perhaps we should not ask for the
formal acquiescence to such necessities.

The development of governance structures over the past four decades,
then, has effectively constrained the president in the entire academic
sphere of an institution's decision making. What John Corson (1975) has
termed "organizational-dualism" was simply two seemingly separate
organizations, each with its own process of decision making. One was
the academic organization with its complex of faculty committees; the
other was the business and operational organization, portrayed in organizational charts and seemingly functioning on bureaucratic or scaler
principles. In halcyon days, the academic organization assumed that the
business and operational organization existed to facilitate the work of the
faculty. In recent years, some faculty, at least, regard the facilitator as
having become the dictator. At the least, it seems clear that such divisions
in a higher education institution between the academic and the bureaucratic are false and that *all* decision making about one "component"
affects all other decision making. For one group to have authority over
educational matters and another group to have authority over budget
matters is at the heart of this matter. The president cannot dictate educational matters, the faculty governance structures cannot determine

budget decisions, except indirectly. Adam Yarmolinsky (1975) has referred to this disjunction as leading to "institutional paralysis." As for the power of the administration, he says:

> No institution in the United States puts more constraints on its administration than a university. The administration cannot hire or fire a faculty member on its own initiative. It cannot initiate a new course offering, or modify or abandon an old one. It cannot determine the requirements for completion of a course of study, or decide whether or not a student has met those requirements. And, in most cases, it can neither admit nor dismiss a student (pp. 61-62).

Disparate Demands on the Presidency

A key problem of the president today is how to be accountable, be in compliance with an assortment of external regulations, satisfy the governing board that he or she is providing leadership to meet the current crises and the needs of the future, and, at the same time, accommodate the expectations of participation and consultation implied by most internal governance structures. The pressures that flow from this quandary are relentless and often disabling. To please the governing board is to displease the faculty. To satisfy the faculty is to engender hostility in the legislature, and on and on.

I illustrate these contradictory expectations by citing an excerpt from the By-Laws of the Board of Regency University System of Illinois (1972) relating to the presidents in their three universities:

> . . . The President is accountable to the Board for every aspect of the conduct and development of the university, including the involvement of faculty, students and staff in the internal governance of the university. In those areas where responsibility is shared he ensures effective and broad based participation in the decision-making process of appropriate components of the university (faculty, students and staff). The president shall be elected by the Board and shall serve at its pleasure.
> . . . In order to promote its responsible self-government, each university shall provide in its constitution for an elected, representative university organization, which shall serve as the primary university body at the institutional level for consultation regarding policy formation. The university constitution may provide for university faculty and administrative staff, student and civil service staff representation on this university body. In the event of serious disagreement between the president and a majority of the members comprising the elected university organization, that organization shall have an opportunity, through a spokesman, to explain its views before the Board at the time the president brings the matter to the Board.

A careful reading of the excerpt makes clear to me the contradiction and the danger. (The Illinois bylaws are not all that different from the bylaws for other state systems.) The president is held accountable for all aspects of the institution, including effective participation by others. Yet the president, despite being the board's agent, is also viewed as one of the two parties to any conflict, with the board as a court of last resort. Instead of linking the president with the board for purposes of managing the board pits the president against the faculty and stands ready to judge disputes. Such an arrangement is not calculated to strengthen a president's resolve to stand up to faculty self-interest; it also automatically undermines the leadership role of the president.

In effect, the president is asked to lead, be responsive, act promptly and decisively, carry out the policies of the board, comply with all directives and regulations of state and federal government, consult widely with a variety of constituencies on campus, consider the advice of relevant constituent groups, and maintain effective relationships with all. These tasks *are* done by many, but no one should overlook the toll it takes on both the individual president and the institution's rational processes.

Collective Bargaining

Perhaps the best illustration of the anomalies of college and university governance is in the advent of faculty collective bargaining. The impact of faculty bargaining on the role of the president has not properly been assessed yet. Its perceived impact in higher education has been studied (Kemerer and Baldridge, 1975). Although the survey data were gathered in 1971, and times have changed greatly, the findings are worth examining.

It was not until 1972 that the AAUP endorsed the principle of faculty collective bargaining. Prior to that time, the field was left to the American Federation of Teachers (AFL-CIO) and the National Education Association. The AAUP had long regarded the labor-management analogy as unprofessional and inappropriate for professors. The 1972 AAUP policy, though, implied that it was possible to have narrow-scope collective bargaining *and* retain shared-authority in governance, including the primary responsibility of faculty for academic policy and personnel matters.

The worsening conditions in higher education that began in the late 1960s and the growth of external influence in institutional governance have led to the spread of faculty collective bargaining. Faculty bargaining has especially increased in public systems of institutions to match growing centralization of authority. Often, the vote by faculty to organize has nothing to do with their attitude toward the campus administration. Rather, it is a political response to the loss of presidential authority on campus.

Each change breeds a change. Deciding which of several events was key in setting up the outcome is like solving the "chicken or egg" conundrum. To have more control over campus decision making, states create systems or statewide boards and coordinating agencies. As these systems, interacting with the executive and legislative branches of state government, intrude on the ability of campus faculty and staff to make their own decisions, faculty members resort to the protection of unionization. If the campus is part of a system, it is likely that collective bargaining will be organized systemwide, as in Florida, New York, New Jersey, Pennsylvania, and many other states. Systemwide collective bargaining requires greater centralization of management authority—and on and on it goes.

Baldridge et al. (1978) observe that "collective bargaining and centralization are ready-made stimulants for each other" (p. 157). In such a situation, as these authors and others have observed, presidents within state systems may become merely "middle management." Yet, their responsibility remains the same to those above, those below, and those outside the campus. It is no wonder, then, that collective bargaining brings added problems to the president in the realm of governance.

I want to close these comments by citing personal interviews I conducted with three presidents reacting to the advent of collective bargaining on their campuses. Two of these are heads of public institutions that are part of increasingly centralized state systems of state colleges and universities. The third is a president of a single, private institution, with its own governing board.

The president of an eastern public college, part of a four-institution system, told me of the start of systemwide faculty collective bargaining in 1976, which was followed by the unionization of the administrative and secretarial staff. There are, therefore, two master contracts negotiated statewide. He told me that at his college, only 11 persons out of the 870 employed were *not* in a union. In the entire state system, only 45 persons out of 2,500 are not in a union. He volunteered that the governor's budget adviser was "the most influential person in the state as far as higher education was concerned, and no one knows him, nor is he held accountable for higher education."

This particular president was concerned about how he, and his board, would work toward overall institution goals when everyone else was a part of a defined interest group, working for their own objectives. Just as centralization encourages "end-runs" to the central administration, collective bargaining had resulted in faculty "end-runs" around the governing board, directly to the governor's office. The union leadership was lobbying directly with the governor and selected members of the legislature, not for the interests of the institution as a whole, but for their own interests.

The other public university president I wish to mention was part of a seven-campus system. When the faculty resorted to collective bargaining it was on a systemwide basis, which greatly increased the role of the central administration. "There was no way I could make a substantive decision without going through Central Administration," he told me. "Everything became centralized under collective bargaining and a coziness developed between the top union guy and the top system guy. The two of them were in control and the presidents were superfluous." Consequently, the presidents spent a great deal of their time going to meetings with each other and the central administration staff to find out what had been agreed to and how they were to act.

This particular president was most upset by the change in the relationship among the various campus entities. Where community members had once shared in governance, they had become adversaries. He cringed at union attempts to put the administration on the defensive. He told me of the enormous time spent in "meet and confer" sessions discussing office hours and contact days. "They would present a problem and then sit in judgment on management's proposal for a solution to the problem. Grievances were filed on every conceivable nit-picking thing." He complained bitterly how all sense of an academic community was lost, citing as one example the union demand that commencement be moved from Saturday to Friday, which the university finally agreed to, rather than pay the faculty for being present. Many parents were unable to attend the ceremony as a result. This president left, dispirited and shaken by his experience, and accepted a presidency in a small, private liberal arts college where the ethos is more collegial than adversarial.

Although found more in public institutions, collective bargaining is also a reality in some private or independent colleges and universities. Often, those most beset by declining enrollment and, thus, financial problems are the first to unionize. I interviewed the president of a private university that had experienced a bitter collective bargaining campaign, protracted negotiations over a first contract, and a difficult faculty strike.

"There is no morality in this union business," the president remarked. He had once been a faculty member and dean at this institution and left to become a president elsewhere. When asked to return to his former institution as president, the governing board told him that a three-year contract would be negotiated prior to his assumption of office. Instead, he arrived to find no contract and the faculty preparing to strike. He also found a serious accumulated deficit and a board expectation that a major retrenchment would be undertaken.

He spoke bitterly of the faculty response to his appeals for unity and assistance in overcoming the financial problems. Instead, he told me, the union fought him every step of the way, taking the position that no faculty should be let go. "They attacked the institution's leadership publicly, refusing to acknowledge that the negative impact this would have on enrollment would also impact on them," he reported. "It was almost barbaric the way this thing operates—scholarly principles, like truth, are out the window. It's almost like a war. Cooperation and understanding are seen as weakness. Victory is the only goal. The sadness is that both sides neutralize one another. No one wins. All energy is dissipated by the confrontation and there's little left for the important things."

He told me of the faculty union's refusal to participate in the long-range planning effort, which had to include program review, resource reallocation, and retrenchment. "They knew that if they participated they'd have to take some responsibility for the outcomes of the planning effort. They preferred to remain free to attack anything we came up with," he said. Not without compassion, he spoke feelingly of the fear and alienation many of his faculty experience—persons with twenty to thirty years toward retirement, nowhere to go, having to go back to teaching survey courses, thinking they are better than that, and in their bitterness lashing out at the institution to which they are irrevocably attached.

He spoke of the enormous spiritual drain he was experiencing as the president. "When I was here before, as the dean, I had the faculty families to my home. We were friends. The shock of having them behave this way is a spiritual drain. Their bitterness causes me enormous stress."

As for the governing board, he said that they had instructed him to "do what you have to do to get us out of this financial mess we're in." When he warned that it might mean a faculty strike, they said they could accept that. "When it came, and they began to get anonymous telephone calls at home, and began to think about their liability, some trustees made end-runs around the president to deal with union leaders. When there is trouble, both the union and the board prefer to blame it on the president."

I make no attempt to answer the quandaries I have described. If I can help to illuminate the phenomenology of the academic presidency, that will suffice. In the next chapter, I comment further on the personal side of the presidency.

8/ The Personal Side of the Presidency

I would not want the reader to think of presidents as unhappy. For the most part, they are healthy, positive, energetic people who regard their work as useful and even important, which view I share.

My focus has necessarily been on the problems associated with the college and university presidency because I believe it important to understand those aspects of the presidency that tend to be dysfunctional. If we in American higher education want effective leadership of our institutions, we must know how to remove barriers to such leadership. Accordingly, I will treat here what David Riesman has referred to as the "vicissitudes" in the lives of college presidents.

Spouse and Family
The recognition that a presidential candidate has a family is first communicated by a governing board during the selection process. Very often, wives of male candidates are invited to accompany their husbands to the final interviews held on a campus. Supposedly, this event provides the wife with an opportunity to see the community and the president's house, but its purpose also includes an opportunity to "look over" the candidate's wife.

There are few married women who are presidents, and, thus, I will not be able to describe the experiences of husbands. Most women presidents are single or widowed. The few who are divorced have experienced some governing board members' concern about the propriety of their social lives or any embarrassment a former spouse might cause.

Except for those men who are priests, the typical male college or university president is married and has a family. The wife is expected to play a role associated with a kind of "first lady" stereotype, although that is rapidly changing in these times. Nevertheless, residential colleges and, particularly, church-related colleges, may place great stress on the charm and cooperativeness of a candidate's wife in making a final decision on selecting a president. In such institutions especially, the president's wife is considered a part of a "team." She is expected to play hostess to a variety of constituencies. The rationale for the provision of a president's house, on campus, is associated with such expectations. This rationale is also true in many public higher education institutions.

Most male presidents know how important a role a wife can play. They are often a link to the broader community, crucial to the success of fund-raising events held on campus, and a source of "intelligence," or feedback, from faculty wives and the wives of governing board members. A single woman president once complained to me of her lack of someone to play this crucial role for her:

> The president's wife is the main conduit of gossip and useful information. She goes out with faculty wives, donor wives, and trustee wives. The whole social structure here is set up to foster that kind of activity. The hardest part of my job is my lack of time to play the wife's social role.

Until fairly recently, wives were not able to resist the traditional role expectations. To do so would have meant the inability of a husband to assume a presidency. That is not to say that many women do not enjoy being "first lady," but the matter of choice did not really exist.

Muriel Beadle (1972), wife of the former president of the University of Chicago, wrote of her own thoughts after returning home with her husband from a presidential interview with the governing board:

> For my part, the idea of running that house was appalling. A thousand faculty wives to get to know. Eight thousand students. Goodness knows what other responsibilities. At Caltech, I had observed Doris DuBridge's activities with sympathy, and I doubted that I could be as consistently nice as she was to people I didn't like very much. Given my inability to dissemble, I'd surely lose the University some multimillion-dollar gift by insulting a potential donor. I am an activist; could I restrict myself to non-controversial kinds of activism? And I detest cocktail parties. What the University of Chicago needed, I was thinking as we flew back to California that night, was a First Lady who had more social savvy than I had (p. 5).

A more detailed study of the satisfactions and frustrations of presidents' wives was conducted by Marguerite Walker Corbally (1977), the wife of the former president of the University of Illinois. Over two hundred wives of male presidents responded to her questionnaire, which covered a broad range of topics—from who provides the china and silver for entertaining to a "frustration" scale. While we know of "two-career families," she describes the uniqueness of "two-person careers."

There is no doubt in my mind that community and governing board expectations are changing and will continue to change regarding the role of presidents' wives (or husbands). Younger women are less willing to spend their lives pursuing other people's goals and dutifully serving in roles they find uncomfortable. As one of the wives states in the Corbally study,

> I suspect that most of us [presidents' wives] resent many times being an unpaid adjunct of our husbands, often ignored as to ability and intelligence no matter what his job. I do wish I could stay around long enough to see what women's lib makes of our problems in another generation or so (p. 128).

A few of the new presidents I interviewed in 1976 told me that their wives were career professionals and had full-time careers outside their homes. That reality is, of course, difficult when the time comes for a husband to move elsewhere for a presidency. In these cases, governing boards had been told that conventional hostess expectations would have to be altered and that funds would have to be provided for housekeeping duties that might have been provided free by a wife. If a candidate was attractive enough, some offers of help were received for locating work for a wife in a new city.

Any expectations of a governing board about the role of the wife and the use of the president's house should be made clear to each finalist and his wife. If a wife intends to work outside the home and will resist being drawn into the social activities of an institution, that should be made known also. The new president is a part of a family unit. If there is unhappiness, resentment, and strain in that family unit, no one can benefit and all will suffer.

One could also write an extensive volume on the difficulties of raising children in the goldfish bowl of a president's house on a campus. Suffice it to say, that too should be a matter of sensitive concern on the part of a governing board.

Accordingly, the sensitivities, concerns, and expectations about such matters should reveal themselves at the time a president is being appointed. Governing boards interviewing candidates should not take the wives for granted as merely adjuncts to their husbands. If there are small children in the family, an offer to pay child care expenses for a lengthy visit would be in order. If there are school-age children in the family, anticipation of such needs and information about schools should be forthcoming. Recognition of a president's spouse and family needs and the importance of a president's personal life is more than simple courtesy or etiquette. The well-being of these other people in the president's life is crucial to effectiveness in the presidency.

When a person is deciding to take a presidency, he (or she) is also deciding to uproot children from familiar surroundings and friends. A wife may have to give up a job and perhaps tenure on a faculty somewhere else. There will be new pressures and some of these will be viewed with realistic apprehension. Will there be any privacy for one's family life? How long is the presidency likely to last and will that necessitate another move? Anyone who is oblivious to such matters is driven by naked ambition and may not make a good president.

Compensation

The mythology of being "called" to serve in a presidency often results in a glossing over of financial considerations, retirement benefits, and compensation. In the glow of having been chosen, many a candidate makes assumptions that are later mistaken. It may appear crass to raise questions of one's personal status and security when asked to be leader of a noble cause but a candidate who fails to discuss these matters often has regrets that could have been prevented.

To an assistant professor, a president's salary might seem large and even out of proportion. Yet, when compared to chief executive officers of business organizations, they are less than one-half the salary of people with comparable positions. Bowen (1978) has conducted a study of academic compensation in which he concludes that academic administrators are paid "markedly less" than their counterparts in business. The comparisons, he says, "raise serious questions about the adequacy of administrative compensation in higher education" (p. 57).

Obviously, people become educators for reasons other than financial gain and stock options. Yet, salaries are often lower than is sensible, due to tradition or to written or unwritten rules that tie a president's salary to a ceiling below the governor of a state. Governors' salaries are often unrealistically low, for political or other, nonmarket, reasons. If one is in a system, the head of which must be paid less than the governor, the salaries of the campus presidents may be woefully low. There may be no incentive to giving up a professorship or deanship to assume higher responsibilities.

Beyond salary, other financial pressures impinge on academic presidents more than is generally realized. They may be at the peak of their earning power, yet they have no job security and no one to fight for their financial interests. Also, presidents are expected by members of the general community to contribute to charity, join various organizations, and the like. Frequently a president must subsidize the entertainment responsibilities associated with the president's role.

One usually hears that a president's compensation includes various perquisites, including living in the President's House. Often, however, living in that house is a financial burden and a number of presidents I have interviewed expressed the desire to live off campus in their own homes for many reasons. Not owning your own home in these inflationary times means tax disadvantages plus no growing equity for the future. When it comes time to depart one's presidency, the disadvantage of not owning a home becomes all too apparent. Additionally, many presidents have to spend their own money to make a president's house livable. College-owned housing is seen as public, rather than private. Various events in the house must be scheduled, from alumni teas to faculty receptions. Strangers are put up, upon the recommendation of trustees or political leaders. If public funds support housekeeping or maintenance, there is the usual political outcry at budget time about the president living in a "mansion with servants" at taxpayers expense. I know of very few presidents who do not wish they could be out of this kind of controversy. A few quotations from wives in the Corbally study will illustrate:

> I previously lived in a "state-owned" house and found the experience so distasteful from the viewpoint of family and personal privacy that I resolved never to take another job which required the sacrifice of one's own life to the public to that extent. My children were constantly reminded about the amount of light, heat, etc., that the state was providing for us and when visitors came to our official residence their behavior was appalling. Frequently people opened closets, invaded the third floor, etc. (p. 89).

> We can't save money because every fund-raising group expects a generous donation, and my husband raises faculty salaries before he touches his own. But we can't ask others to contribute to our school if we don't contribute to their pet causes (symphony, art museum, charities, etc.) (p. 129).

> I find that I am one of our college's prime benefactors. I pay for coffee, nuts, soda, breakage and damage, tips to delivery people, furniture cleaning and repair, floor waxing, and a cleaning lady to help me restore the house to livability (p. 121).

> The house provided no advantage. We were expected to use it as a reception room or motel for visiting dignitaries. We eventually moved out (p. 91)!

The Unspoken Feelings

The presidency has always been a difficult and lonely job but its importance was not challenged. Today, the job is even more difficult because of greater personal insecurity, less authority, and more controversy. Self-interest politics may make the next decade far more difficult for presidents than the past decade.

Through the 1950s, the presidency was seen as a public affairs position. Father Hesburgh of the University of Notre Dame still plays such a role on the national and world scene, but there are no other presidents I can name. Yale University President Kingman Brewster and Vanderbilt University Chancellor Alexander Heard have played such roles—they are from the private sector. Clark Kerr has played a significant public policy role, but only after leaving the presidency of the University of California. For the most part, in the decade past, the position has been occupied by persons skilled in coping, negotiating, and obtaining resources in a volatile climate. This reality is entirely understandable, of course.

From the mid-1960s on, many presidents experienced campus disruption and violence; public criticism; the "demands" of various interest groups, minorities, and women; financial crises; attacks on the value of higher education itself; widespread intrusions by state and federal government; and, perhaps most distressing, the experience of dealing with one's faculty as adversaries during collective bargaining negotiations and strife.

Translating this litany into the experiential impact it has had on the lives of individual presidents so others can appreciate it is my purpose.

Presidents, while gregarious in politically effective ways, are often lonely people. Often, only another president can understand a colleague's experience for it is difficult to share with others. This difficulty is not a contemporary phenomenon only. Writing his thoughts, William Rainey Harper, first president of the University of Chicago, penned these words in 1904.

> . . . Another feeling which gradually grows upon the occupant of the presidential chair is that of great loneliness—the feeling of separation from all his fellows. At certain times he realizes that in all truth he *is* alone; for those who are ordinarily close to him seem to be, and in fact are, far away. On occasions of this kind courage is needed; strength, of a peculiar character. An ordinary man—and after all the college president is an ordinary man—cannot thus be cut off from his associates and fail to experience the sorrow of such separation. The college presidency means the giving up of many things, and, not the least among them, one's most intimate friendships. Moreover, this feeling of separation, of isolation, increases with each recurring year, and, in spite of the most vigorous effort, it comes to be a thing of permanence. This is inevitable, and it is as sad as it is inevitable (p. 183).

I do not wish to portray the president of a college or university as a paragon of virtue who ought to be above the sounds, smells, and feel of the everyday fray that most of us experience. Yet most people do not experience the leader's role, the projection of others' frustrations and transference, the lacerating impact of being unable to convey to others that some problems are simply unsolvable by the president. Being a president is to feel exaggerated and false admiration about one's presumed power and graciousness bordering on obsequiousness for what one may be presumed to be able to do on another's behalf. Yet being a president is to feel anger and hate, too, fantastically projected on to the leader who seemingly will not make poverty and ignorance disappear and peace reign in the world.

Presidents do not tell people what it feels like to have antiwar protesters hurl obscenities at them because they will not make war go away, as they defend free speech and association on their campuses; or of the need for police protection for their families because of threats to their physical well-being; of bomb threat telephone calls; disruptions of honors convocations when parents expect respect for the achievements of their sons and daughters. I once closed down a college switchboard during a commencement exercise in 1970 with the directive to my staff, "I do not want to receive word of any bomb threats during the graduation ceremony."

Presidents do not tell what it feels like to work for affirmative action, to override all criticism in bringing in minority students through special admissions and financial aid, and then have such staff and students organize a public protest, with mass-media coverage, to attack you as a symbol of institutional racism, and to demand more jobs and scholarships for minorities. "Nothing personal," someone once remarked to me on such an occasion.

Presidents do not tell what it feels like to be threatened by a board member, to be vilified in the student newspaper, to deal with an arsonist, call in police, or explain to the governor why an emergency situation could not have been anticipated. Defending *the* faculty, when some are slothful and fakers; defending *the* students, when some are beyond any seeming redemption; these are necessary and everyday responsibilities, at least in the public presidency.

Presidents do not tell what it feels like to fail in meeting fund-raising goals because of a recession or a falling stock market, and have to freeze salaries and let some staff go; or fail to convince the governor or the legislature of the worthiness of an appropriation request crucial to maintaining the status quo. I once quoted a sensitive passage of poetry from Gibran during a fall convocation and an English professor vehemently told me that if I meant what that passage said, I should see to it that his salary was raised—otherwise I was a phony.

In these hard times of resource reallocation, it no longer is a watching game to see who or what is rewarded. Rather, faculty and staff watch to see who gets hurt as programs are reviewed for reductions and trade-offs. You may have to take your choice of continuing to exploit a grossly overworked business faculty, supplemented with "moonlighters," or become an enemy of the humanities by taking away some of their positions. And so it goes—needing a foreign policy regarding South Africa; trying to find money for women's athletics; arguing with the system office staff about their method of computing allocations for part-time adult students; defending a request for support funds for basic skills as you try to explain grade inflation; assuring the faculty that you will await their recommendations before deciding, as you assure the legislative finance committee that you are firmly and fully in charge of your campus; and defending your use of qualitative peer judgments in faculty promotions, as the federal investigator asks you to show cause why you should not be deemed guilty of discrimination.

One successful state college president I know resigned after ten years of service and started farming. In his letter of resignation, he cited the increasing red tape and growing bureaucracy as frustrations no longer tolerable to him as an educator. Pointing to a recent biweekly meeting agenda of the chancellor and system presidents, he recounted,

> . . . a half-day was spent mainly on reviewing the latest rules and regulations, a briefing on newly issued requirements for the handicapped, an analysis of the impact of new federal laws on staff retirements, pending costs of social security changes, technical adjustments in health insurance administration, and the status of numerous lawsuits and court decisions. There was no time to discuss educational matters.

What to Do Next

From my personal interviews with new presidents, I have had recounted to me numerous illustrations of the superhuman effort put forth in the first presidential year. All the presidents I talked with had stretched themselves to get to know everyone, accept all speaking engagements, visit with students and alumni, win the respect of the faculty, and on and on. There is a feeling of elation that one has survived it all. For many, there was a joy in accomplishment and in having discovered one's own strengths and capacities. Yet, there is the beginning of a new and sobering thought—how long can I keep this up, and what will I do next?

To stay on the job means compromise. One sees already the resistance to one's goals, the problems that lie ahead, the staff that will need to be changed or converted. How much more responsibility are you willing to take? If you really shake up the place, bring in new people, start some major battles—you must be prepared to stay awhile or leave the place in a shambles with your own reputation at stake. If you compromise, convert staff to your way of thinking, make do with things, how long can you keep up the pace? What will you do next?

It is rare in these times for a president to serve more than ten years. Five years is probably closer to the average. Presidents often give up tenure or security when they move to a presidency. In some systems, such as that of the University of Wisconsin, "normal" retirement for the president and chancellors is set for age sixty-two, while it is seventy for faculty.

My experience reveals that presidents, in their third or fourth year in office, worry about lack of tenure a great deal. This concern is especially poignant at age fifty-seven or fifty-eight, when starting a new career may be precluded and remaining as president indefinitely seems precarious indeed. There are health concerns and wonderment about whether or not a governing board would be compassionate and provide a graceful exit if one had to leave office.

Some presidents are crushed by the idea of leaving the presidency. They have come to identify themselves and their worth with the office. They *have* to be president, which does not serve an institution very well. Despite the problems of the presidency, it is probably the most challenging, demanding, and what could be called "peak" experience one can have. Probably no other position exists that will again engage a person as has a college presidency.

As the role of president becomes more and more temporary and lacking in security, we in higher education will need to discover incentives to attract the quality of leadership so greatly needed. Increasingly, disincentives are complicating our choices. People committed to humane values and human growth must be the leaders of our educational enterprise. If people with such commitments are driven away from such posts, we will be in danger of making true the charges that we are running factories, not schools.

9/ Assessing Presidential Effectiveness

Presidents are judged almost every day by almost everyone, whether they like that or not. It is in the nature of the role of leader and manager or, for that matter, almost any role which encompasses the assumption of significant responsibilities.

Because I believe that colleges and universities, as organizations, have multiple and ambiguous criteria for success, the presidents of such organizations also inherit that complexity and ambiguity when it comes to judging or assessing their own success. It follows, then, that a great deal of understanding is necessary if one is to evaluate presidential effectiveness.

Since I last wrote on this topic (Kauffman, 1978), the subject of presidential assessment and the evaluation of administrators generally have become of great interest. As the student protest era led to a greater emphasis on student evaluation of courses and teachers, that emphasis escalated to teacher evaluation of administrators. Spurred on by demands for accountability and improved management, performance auditing, and the like, it was not long before it seemed appropriate to focus on presidential evaluation. Accordingly, there has been a rush of publications on the topic, much of it from the research and measurement community. Several publications are worthy of the reader's attention. These include a volume by Charles H. Farmer (1979); a book edited by Charles F. Fisher (1978); a book by G. Lester Anderson (1977); and a chapter by Barry Munitz in a 1980 book of the Association of Governing Boards of Universities and Colleges. The most recent look at how presidential assessment is actually conducted, when it is done, is detailed in a forthcoming book by John Nason, to be published by the Association of Governing Boards in 1980.

For the most part, presidents themselves have been silent on the subject, including those presidents who have been "assessed." Yet the presidents I have interviewed are wary, and properly so, of the rush to apply techniques of personnel evaluation and survey research to their difficult, many-dimensional roles. In 1975, presidents belonging to the American Association of State Colleges and Universities adopted a policy statement that contained their own recommended guidelines for evaluation. Those guidelines reflect the delicate nature of presidential leadership and the assessment of such a role.

Purpose of Evaluation

What is the purpose of evaluation or assessment and why the concern with this subject?

In its most rational form, performance review, assessment, or evaluation are legitimate and expected personnel functions. They are not meant to be public relations exercises, political acts, or morality plays. Evaluation is necessary and functional. As with other personnel functions, evaluation's purpose is to improve performance and productivity. Ideally, then, evaluation contains elements of feedback and coaching within a mutual-benefit context. Through evaluation, everyone is aided to do a better job, increased job satisfaction occurs, and the organization benefits as well. In any profit-making organization, a functional personnel operation would itself be evaluated on how well it met such goals.

If one is to evaluate presidential assessment, then, the criteria would have to include the following: Does the assessment process help attract and retain presidents of the highest quality? Does it help improve their performance, their productivity and job satisfaction? Does it aid in the retention of excellent presidents and assist in the rapid weeding out of those who are not suitable for the organization's needs? Is it regarded as legitimate by those affected by it? If an institution's presidential assessment does not aim at such goals, it must be regarded as dysfunctional. Whether to assess is not the question. How to assess college and university presidents is the issue.

If the role of president is one of service, and if the president "serves at the pleasure of the Board," then it is the governing board which must assume full responsibility for the adequacy of presidential assessment. Often, the governing board itself is a major factor in the president's effectiveness or lack of effectiveness. It is how the board and president work together that may be the crucial determinant of presidential success. Therefore, the governing board must also examine itself as it assesses its chief executive officer—the president.

Evaluation and Governance

To be effective, assessment must be carried out in an atmosphere of mutual trust and benefit. Otherwise, a lack of candor and a withholding of vital information can occur. Any human transaction affecting a college or university that is treated with cynicism or deprecation erodes other transactions that may be crucial to the health of the institution. For this reason, I do not recommend the imposition of an assessment process without the participation of those to be assessed. A governing board that is cynical about the process is just as harmful as a president who resists assessment.

In chapter 7, I described the interaction of the presidency and various forms of institutional governance, which I believe to be important in presidential assessment. If one is to draw a continuum of governance processes, the two polar extremes would constitute a "trust" model and a "distrust" model. That is, at one extreme, authority would be commensurate with responsibility and presidents would be expected to use judgment, discretion, and authority and stand ready to be accountable for their performance. The "distrust" model, however, introduces a wide variety of actors: pre-auditors, anonymous persons in various state personnel, budget, and purchasing agencies, and several layers of authority intervening and interacting on decisions. Authority is not commensurate with responsibility and accountability.

The "trust" model is more likely to occur in private or single-campus institutions; the "distrust" model of governance is more likely to be found in public institutions and especially in multicampus state systems. For these reasons, therefore, I think it is easier to create effective presidential assessment practices at a Haverford College and a Willamette University than for the Pennsylvania State Colleges or the State University System of Florida.

The Politics of Evaluation

A politics of evaluation needs to be considered in presidential assessment. In the public sector, politics is often the motivating force for initiating a process of formal evaluation of presidents. Evaluation can be a symbolic act, with accompanying posturing about tough management and accountability. The rush to become draped with the latest management fashion may not, however, be accompanied by a thoughtful assessment process that others will have to implement and live with. I was once asked to serve as consultant to a board of regents that had promulgated a policy mandating the formal evaluation of its president and chancellors and then, when the time came, saw how difficult it would be to implement. The president himself, whose staff had prepared the policy for board approval, backed off when it came time to implement the plan. His remark to me was, "Do you know how difficult it is to get a good chancellor? My obligation is to hold on to good people, not run them off."

Partisan politics may also be a factor in creating evaluation machinery in some public systems. When a president may be removed from office by the governor, as is true for state college presidents in Pennsylvania, one tends to view formal evaluation programs with a properly wary eye.

Florida offers a good example of the point I seek to emphasize. In the face of threats by the Florida legislature to create a statutory provision for the formal evaluation of the state university system administrators, the governing board of that nine-university system established, in 1974, a formal performance review system for its presidents and chancellor that is linked with a five-year term appointment. The former chancellor of the Florida system, Robert B. Mautz (1979) wrote recently that he "believed then and emphasizes now that such reviews are inappropriate; as they are now structured, reviews do not benefit the institution, and they may obstruct exercise of positive leadership" (Tucker and Mautz, p. 255). One may respectfully ask why counterproductive evaluation procedures get institutionalized against the better judgment of those responsible for the leadership of our colleges and universities. On many occasions I have heard presidents and governing board members say that the sole reason for their policy was the political reality that necessitated a public stand for such evaluation.

Public institutions, then, and especially public systems of institutions, have unique political pressures that impact on performance review programs. The sense of those pressures may force presidents and trustees to come to grips with unpleasant tasks they would prefer to postpone. Those same pressures, though, may trigger responses that meet today's problems but become increasingly dysfunctional as time goes on. The latter must be resisted.

I do not deny that public university systems may, for political reasons, require a visible evaluation program for its top administrators. But if this is necessary, there is all the more reason for a sensitive process that rewards and reinforces excellent performance and enables the system to get and keep superior executives. Any personnel process that does not achieve this goal is a failure.

Term Appointments and Evaluation

Formal evaluation procedures, requiring periodic performance review of presidents, are often tied to term appointments. The model often cited is that of the State University of New York system (SUNY). In that system the initial appointment is for five years. Those presidents desiring a second appointment of five years must undergo an evaluation.

The implication of the term appointment is that a temporary period of leadership should not become indefinite without some review of the president's performance and suitability for the future needs of the institution. Thus, the formal evaluation process, linked to a second appointment, often carries with it the connotation of a "pass-fail" assessment.

If such an exercise is carried out in public or during collective bargaining, it may end the usefulness of a president. It also compromises the authority of the governing board, at whose pleasure the president serves.

The one major element of the SUNY system that many public systems do not have is the simultaneous appointment to the presidency and a tenured professorship within that system. This arrangement enables governing board members to attract good people and provides a dignified exit for those presidents who decline reappointment or are counseled out of seeking another term. Academic leaders planning to adopt a combined term appointment and formal evaluation process for renewal must take into account the vital need to provide such financial security and/or means for graceful exiting. Otherwise, presidents must choose between doing what is right for their institutions or protecting their own job security. Management should not place chief executive officers in such a quandary.

Term appointments must be tied to some kind of escape system that provides a dignified exit without undue economic penalties. A president should not be expected to expend him- or herself for the good of the cause while everyone else is protected by job security, tenure, or due process considerations.

My major concern, however, is that we should *separate* the performance review process from the governing board's responsibility for deciding to retain or let go a president. Failure to make this distinction undermines both the governing board and the president.

If the board acts as though it does not know whether or not to keep its president, the legitimacy of presidential leadership is eroded. If the board always reappoints a president following a formal evaluation, then the legitimacy of the evaluation is eroded. If the board wishes to reject a president's request for reappointment and, in the course of a public evaluation, some dissident faculty faction demands he or she be fired, the board is in a public posture of seeming to give in to such political pressures.

My view is that the review should be separate from any reappointment outcome. If a board has lost confidence in its president, it should tell that president that he or she will not be reappointed. If the board has confidence in its president, the review should be regarded as the gathering of necessary feedback and intelligence to enable the president to do a better job. Above all, formal evaluation should not be allowed to turn into a public *trial*. If that occurs, the president is doomed, no matter what the outcome is.

Presidents are not in a popularity contest. Under collective bargaining, there are political reasons why a faculty must oppose the president as spokesperson for management. One beleaguered president expressed the dilemma to me this way:

> Perhaps the most difficult problem for the president is the realization that
> if he does his job well under contemporary conditions, he almost
> certainly will be disliked by faculty. Indeed, a trustee once said to me

that if the faculty praised my performance, he would be suspicious that I
was not carrying out the wishes of the board or pursuing the well-being
of the institution as a whole. I suspect that in all but the most well-
endowed institutions today, faculty desires are at cross-purposes with
institutional well-being and the president is fated to be at cross-purposes
with the professional group from which he is drawn.

The Governing Board and Evaluation
I believe that a president's performance cannot be separated from a
governing board's performance. Although the roles are definitely not the
same, they are inextricably related. They affect one another in countless
ways.

If a board has an effective relationship with its president, and does its
job well, that fact will help make the president effective. If the board
mistrusts a president, does not have confidence in his or her recommendations, or communicates, however subtly, its discomfort over presidential behavior, that reality will spill over onto presidential effectiveness.
The board cannot separate itself from the president. The president is the
agent of the board. If the board is unhappy with the performance of the
president, it must confront that fact at once. It must not allow itself to
become a jury, judging the president impartially, as it would judge disputes
between the president and other constituent groups. If the board believes
that the president is not carrying out its policies and will, and cannot do
so, it must replace the president.

From this viewpoint, then, I believe that presidential assessment requires a review of the president's relationship to the governing board and
an assessment of the board's performance as well. The Association of
Governing Boards (1976) has provided guidelines for board self-assessment and they may be useful when undertaking such a task.

The Problem of Criteria for Evaluation
Assessment of performance presupposes some rational process in which
there are criteria or objectives against which performance can be measured. To determine how well someone is doing, some standard must exist
for comparisons. At the very least, one ought to have some agreed-upon
objectives for successful performance that serve as the foundation for the
inquiry.

I asked new presidents completing their first year as presidents by what
criteria they thought their success would be judged. Most said that no
clear criteria were known to them and some spoke strongly of what the
criteria ought to be. Others expressed their disappointment that no one
seemed to care about this question.

The new president in one state system said, "When the board hired
me, they told me that they wanted me to be a strong president and a strong
leader. If I get any negative evaluation it will be because I did just that.

There is real irony in this. My political contacts, my lobbying for my campus, my leadership and aggressiveness, are now being resented." He reported that a gross kind of evaluation goes on in his system, in which campus presidents are divided into two groups—okay and not okay—on the basis of their submitting to central administration. After complaining about the dynamics of the situation in which he found himself, he remarked, "But I don't think they will evaluate me at all, which is the real tragedy."

Others complained in a similar vein. One said that "unless something happens to educate the board, they simply won't have any basis for evaluating the president. The board now has no way of knowing what presidents ought to be doing or how well they are doing it."

In another university system, a new chancellor stated that he wanted to be judged on the effectiveness of the administrative organization he was building. However, his real concern was with the central administration in the system. "I am tough," he said. "They'll resent my fighting for my campus all the time. They'll get you if you keep fighting them— especially if you win some." He, too, added as an afterthought, "But I suppose the worst thing is that I may not be judged at all by central administration."

In still another system, a campus president commented on the absence of real communication about objectives and criteria for evaluation. He emphasized the importance of the evaluation process. "The specific objectives or criteria chosen may be less important than the process itself," he observed. "The process of thinking through the long-term goals of the institution together—the president and the board—that's the real value."

Some of the public university presidents were apprehensive about the emphasis that faculty would place on their ability to get sufficient appropriations from the state or from their system. No matter what else they are able to accomplish, these presidents feel that the faculty will judge them on appropriations. "Do they kill the messenger who brings bad news?" was the way one president phrased the concern.

State systems that have programs of formal evaluation for their presidents express their performance objectives or criteria very differently. Some are stated in general terms, similar to the criteria or qualifications used in the selection of presidents. Others are detailed almost in the form of behavioral objectives to be measured. In the following pages are described those criteria specified in the formal evaluation programs of the SUNY system, the Florida University system, and the Pennsylvania State College system.

State University of New York (SUNY)
By the SUNY performance criteria (1977), presidents are judged according to the extent to which they fulfill "those responsibilities of the chief

administrative officer of the campus, as defined by the Board of Trustees in 1976." It is made clear that the performance review is a trustee function and that the process is distinct from the search process for new presidents. Rather than develop new or special criteria for evaluation, then, the statement of "responsibilities" provides the criteria against which a president's effectiveness is reviewed. That statement follows:

Responsibilities
The chief administrative officer of each college shall be responsible to the Chancellor and the Board of Trustees for, and shall administer, the college for which he serves, and shall promote its development and effectiveness. He shall supervise the members of the professional and nonacademic staff of such college. He shall appoint or recommend to the Chancellor and the Board of Trustees persons for appointment as members of the professional staff of the college. He shall prepare and recommend the annual budget request of the college. He shall report and make recommendations to the Chancellor and the Board of Trustees and the college council concerning the operation, plans and development of the college. He shall make all appointments of employees to positions at his college in the classified service of the civil service of the State (p. 8).

State University System of Florida

The Board of Regents of the State University System of Florida has statutory responsibility for the appointment of the president of each of the nine universities in that system. Chapter 6C-4, of *the Rules of the Department of Education, Board of Regents*, specifies the Regents' rules regarding the presidents and 6C-4.02 mandates the formal evaluation requirement.

In the Board of Regents Policy Guidelines for the performance review of its presidents the following criteria are listed under the heading "Standards of Evaluations."

The following factors will constitute the basic criteria for evaluating each President through the means of interviews and questionnaires:
A. performance of assigned responsibilities as a measure of his ability to perform stated objectives
B. quality of relations with students, faculty, and staff
C. ability to resolve conflicts and grievances satisfactorily as well as initiate action to reduce the causes for grievances
D. ability to make decisions, the degree of acceptance of decisions, and the manner in which they are carried out
E. ability to select and retain qualified personnel, whose job performance would indicate the ability of the president to recruit qualified personnel
F. ability to evaluate and organize staff to obtain maximum performance
G. adequacy and accuracy of planning
H. initiation of studies, reviews, and evaluations of policies and procedures employed at the institution

I. quality of written and oral communication, including accuracy, adequacy, and timeliness
J. budget preparation and execution in accordance with policy
K. cost control and productivity
L. ability to apply and creatively use statutes and regulations relating to higher education
M. adequacy of academic programs to serve needs of institution's appropriate, target population.

State Colleges of Pennsylvania

On July 13, 1978, the Board of Directors of the State Colleges of Pennsylvania approved detailed criteria for presidential evaluation (1978). Four general areas were identified:

A. Administrative Leadership and Management
B. Academic Leadership and Management
C. Internal Relationships
D. External Relationships.

The board's statement then explicates the process and the criteria with the following directions:

In each of these general categories evaluators should indicate the President's greatest weaknesses and greatest strengths and state the basis for those conclusions. Evaluators should also make suggestions for assisting the President to improve his or her performance.

The following statements are representative of those which may be addressed in each evaluation area. The statements should not be construed as a rigid checklist but as suggestions for the types of issues which should be raised by evaluation committees.

A. *Administrative Leadership and Management*
1. The goals which were established at the time of appointment have been fulfilled.
2. An understanding of budgeting, accounting, and fiscal management procedures has been demonstrated.
3. Budgeting priorities and realistic controls which enable institutional needs to be met while maintaining a balanced budget have been effectively established.
4. The efforts of various segments of the staff in meeting institutional goals have been effectively directed and coordinated.
5. Responsibility and authority have been effectively delegated without abdicating the President's own responsibility.
6. The ability to administer the institution in a dynamic and productive manner while observing the restraints of government and system control and available resources has been demonstrated.
7. Qualified faculty, administrators, and other staff members with potential for productivity and professional growth have been appointed.

8.   Leadership in developing and maintaining physical facilities conducive to wholesome living and learning has been provided.

B.   *Academic Leadership and Management*
1.   Respect for high standards of scholarship in teaching and research has been encouraged.
2.   Leadership and direction in defining and adapting the mission, goals and objectives of the institution have been provided.
3.   Effective leadership in the various facets of long range planning for the institution has been provided.
4.   Responsive academic leadership to societal and students needs has been provided.
5.   Curriculum revision and improvement has been encouraged.
6.   Effective involvement of faculty, administrative staff members, and students in curriculum development has been encouraged.
7.   The President participates in local, state, or national professional organizations.

C.   *Internal Relationships*
1.   A consciousness of common purpose among the diverse constituencies of the institution has been promoted.
2.   The various segments of the college have been dealt with even-handedly with the best interests of the college at the forefront.
3.   A level of academic freedom appropriate to a community of scholars has been encouraged.
4.   A sincere interest in, sensitivity to and understanding of the needs and concerns of faculty, students and staff has been demonstrated.
5.   Firmness, objectivity and impartiality in carrying out presidential responsibilities have been demonstrated.
6.   The President has supported college activities through participation and attendance.
7.   A wholesome working relationship with faculty, student and staff governance groups and organizations on the campus has been maintained.
8.   The President has the respect and confidence of the college or university constituencies.
9.   All segments of the college or university have been properly informed concerning issues which may or should be of interest to them and the President has been open to suggestions from all campus constituencies.
10. The professional growth and development of the staff members have been encouraged.
11. Student participation in campus governance has been encouraged.

D.   *External Relationships*
1.   A positive and constructive relationship with state and local government has been maintained.
2.   An atmosphere of openness and candor with news media has been maintained.

3. Positive town-gown relationships have been promoted.
4. The President has participated in community activities.
5. The President has the respect of the community.
6. The President has secured the interest and support of alumni.
7. The President has been an effective spokesman in interpreting the college or university to the several publics which the college or university serves and upon which it must depend for support.

Who Participates and How?

Among the many issues involved in presidential evaluation are the following: should subordinates and constituent groups participate; should evaluative comments be attributable or not; should the process be confidential or not? (Formal evaluations in public institutions tend to involve constituent participation. If one is not careful, this participation can turn the process into a circus; opinion polls and public hearings can make the event resemble a trial.)

Should individuals be allowed to volunteer negative statements, under the cloak of anonymity? If so, how is one to weigh such statements or respond to them? If not, can one get adequate information without anonymity? What are the rights of the president who is being evaluated? Does he or she have any rights to face an accuser?

I believe that the process must be conducted on a confidential basis. Anonymous material should not be considered legitimate, but those conducting the assessment should be able to pledge confidentiality to those offering observations.

As for constituent participation, I do not believe that faculty, students, or staff have the knowledge or competence to evaluate a president, nor should they be expected to. Yet, some consultation with representatives of such groups may prove beneficial and useful. The context of such consultation then is what is so crucial to its success. If the context is negative—"we don't know whether to keep the president or not; what do you think?"—the consultation product will not be useful. If the context is positive—"In what areas do you think the president needs to give more effort or a higher priority?"—the product can be useful. But we are talking about perceptions that can be instructive for the president. Gathering such perceptions is *not* to be confused with evaluation of presidential performance.

The Montana University System has had a formal evaluation program for its presidents. Adapted from the SUNY model, without the safety net of tenured professorship and paid study leave provisions, however, it is not greatly respected. One of the senior presidents of the Montana system provided me with a critique of his experience with the evaluation process, and I will cite some of his observations.

It is my understanding that the purpose of any evaluation is to measure performance against a stated norm or set of job expectation descriptors. The purpose is to reward those that are performing above the average and to motivate those performing below the average to improve. It should also motivate those high performers to keep performing at a high level. Often there are financial or other rewards and incentives tied to the evaluation.

My personal observations have been that the evaluation procedures here were hardly carried out in a dignified manner fitting the Office of President, or even of the lowest faculty or staff member. In my naivete, and desire to go along with the evaluation, I agreed to a faculty questionnaire that was geared to elicit only negative comments. The faculty and the president are increasingly adversaries.

My own self-assessment, covering five years of effort, was over sixty pages in length and required considerable effort to prepare. There was no opportunity for me to present it in any formal setting. In fact, its receipt was never acknowledged nor did I receive any word as to anyone's reaction to my self-evaluation.

The above quotation should suffice to indicate the personal hurt that can ensue from faculty evaluation procedures. We must learn from this and not become inured to such hurts.

The Florida Experience

The Florida presidential evaluation program, because of the legal requirements for it and the political pressures that gave rise to it, is highly controversial. I regard it as a good example of how badly the institutionalization of evaluation can become in a large, politicized system. Florida has systemwide collective bargaining plus a "sunshine" law that permits few confidential actions, if any, by state officers, including education administrators. If any two regents talk, that constitutes a meeting. Thus, discussion by a regent committee of the results of an evaluation is considered public information. Presidents in the Florida system do not automatically receive tenured professorships upon appointment as they do in the State University of New York system.

What of the presidents themselves? If we use Florida as an example of formal evaluation and term appointments, invoked largely for symbolic, political reasons, what do we find? The first three presidents who submitted to the formal evaluation process were all reappointed by the board of regents and shortly thereafter submitted their resignations. (One president left for a presidency in another state rather than submit to the evaluation process.) One would have to ask how functional a personnel evaluation system is that waits five years to discharge ineffective executives or drives out those it votes to reappoint.

One president in the Florida system, who upon the successful conclusion of the evaluation process resigned from his presidency, commented to me on the performance review as follows:

This procedure is degrading to the office of the presidency of a university. I have no objection to the president of a university accounting to the board of regents and/or the chancellor with reference to his performance of assigned responsibilities, but I do think that it should be done in such a way as to enhance the office rather than degrade it. After all, the president of a university is the chief administrative arm of the board of regents on that campus. During the coming months in which collective bargaining is to be conducted, the regents need to take every available appropriate step to strengthen the presidencies of the several universities and their administrative staffs.

The Florida system evaluation process is staffed by persons in the system administration office, most of whom have been neither professors nor campus administrators. Thus, they lack sensitivity to the subtle nature of presidential leadership and only gather data through questionnaires and telephone surveys they devise to assess presidential performance. These mechanistic means are unyielding and do not provide a total picture of performance.

For example, a telephone survey of a sample of faculty asks respondents to assess presidential performance on a five-point Likert scale as follows:

1. Almost always
2. Usually
3. Occasionally
4. Seldom
5. Almost never

Illustrative of the survey questions are the following, obtained from an actual questionnaire used in the last two years:

Organizational Management
1. Delegates authority and responsibility adequately.
2. Demonstrates ability to select and retain qualified personnel.
3. Is readily accessible.
4. Maintains a good quality of relations with associates and staff.

Operational Management
5. Provides for the efficient operation of university programs, classes, and services.
6. Implements plans and procedures for the development and improvement of the instructional program of the university.
7. Does a good job of budget preparation and execution.
8. Consistently recommends and implements studies essential to long range planning for the university's operation.

External Relations
9. Actively seeks to create favorable public attitudes towards the university.
10. Seems able to apply and creatively use statutes and regulations relating to higher education for the benefit of the university.

11. Keeps abreast of new developments and innovations in higher
     education.

Overall Atmosphere
12. Adequately keeps the teaching/learning function uppermost in plans
     and action.
13. Inspires confidence.
14. Instills enthusiasm for professional goals.

Human Relations
15. Judges people fairly.
16. Makes sound decisions.
17. Resolves or ameliorates conflict in grievances.
18. Seeks to maintain close working relationships with the faculty.
19. Supports and assists programs for faculty growth and improvement.

Management Style
20. Demonstrates open mindedness, welcomes differences in
     viewpoints.
21. Properly involves relevant persons in planning and decision making.
22. Demonstrates the ability to say "no" effectively.
23. Is generally effective.

A mailed questionnaire, of a similar nature, was also sent to selected
alumni and classified career service employees on the president's campus.

Recently Allan Tucker and Richard B. Mautz (1979), who "helped
inaugurate a program of review of presidential performance" in Florida,
made a statement that best summarizes my position:

> The manner in which presidential evaluations take place almost
> guarantees a dismal rating. Several factors assure this outcome. Few
> members of the university community are able to render an informed
> judgment about the president's total performance. Furthermore, the
> position is such that some dissatisfaction with the president's
> performance is almost inevitable, be he saint or sinner (p. 256).

The SUNY Experience

The presidential evaluation program at SUNY was instituted in 1973. Its
experience may be instructive for all large, public systems of institutions.
It should be re-emphasized that its term appointments and evaluations
are tied to a security system of tenured professorships and paid leaves for
study and renewal. The policy's enlightenment is further reflected in the
continual evaluation of the presidential evaluation process to improve
that process. Murray H. Block, deputy to the chancellor, has chronicled
the various changes made in that program (1979).

In July 1979, new guidelines for the performance review process were
adopted by the SUNY trustees. The guidelines represent several basic
changes from previous practices and they are in a direction I applaud.

One major change is to reduce the time frame for the assessment from ten months to no longer than four months. Further, the president's statement (self-evaluation) is not to exceed twenty pages. Evaluative information must be attributable, which precludes the use of opinion polls and general surveys. But the most significant change, in my view, is the creation of a "visiting team" from a panel of present or former college presidents from outside of the SUNY system to conduct a site visit, speak with appropriate constituent representatives on campus, and conduct the evaluation. This team is analogous to the visiting team used in accreditation. The accreditation visitors are outsiders with sufficient experience to know what to look for and how to corroborate or investigate questionable data.

Final Thoughts on Evaluation

Informal evaluation *must* take place continually between a governing board and a president if both are to be successful in carrying out their responsibilities. This interchange requires candor and openness of communication by both the board and the president. It also requires a willingness on the part of a president to listen and consider suggestions and criticism.

Formal evaluation can serve a useful purpose also, but only when it is done in a proper manner can it be truly functional. It is better not to do formal evaluation if it is not done right.

Done right, formal evaluation involves an assessment of both the board and the president, and especially the quality of their relationships. It involves an examination of governance and especially those aspects of a governance system that get in the way of presidential effectiveness.

It is crucial that the president be willing to participate in any formal assessment and cooperate fully in it. Formal evaluation should not be used as an excuse to terminate a president in whom the board has lost confidence. Such an abdication to others undermines both the board and future presidents. It also undermines the potential utility of formal assessment. Rather, the purpose of performance reviews must be seen as performance improvement. Thus, interviews with key constituent groups would ask for suggestions for improvement, and greater attention, effort, and priority. The result is not only an "inferred" assessment and an "action" agenda, but also a consultative process.

Above all, the evaluation process must not denigrate the office or the person of the president. All too frequently, that is the outcome of the many clumsy attempts at formal evaluation. For this reason, I believe an external consultant must be involved to help conduct the process. Such a person should have had the experience of serving as a president and should be completely acceptable to both the governing board and the president to be assessed.

10/ The President and Educational Leadership

In this essay I have described the college and university presidency as a temporary role of leadership rather than a profession or career. Further, I have shown how that role has been changing as well as the difficulties, constraints, and personal costs involved in being a president. My purpose has been to show the importance of the presidency, not only to our institutions but also to the long-term public welfare.

Observers portray the decade ahead primarily in terms of "decline." Although we may use such descriptors as "steady state" to characterize the quality of the coming years, we know in our hearts that "unsteady" or "turbulent" may be a more fitting description. The reasons for this uncertainty are many.

The conventional assumptions about higher education for the next decade include (1) a decline in the number of students attending college; (2) increasing economic problems due, in part, to energy shortages and costs, resulting in inflation and unemployment; and (3) a lowered sense of the value or priority of support for higher education. There are major studies and books on these three assumptions and I will not explore these in detail here. Yet it is important to point out that changing demographic facts will not have a uniform impact on all institutions. In some areas of the country, the numbers of eighteen year olds will increase in the 1980s. In some sun-belt states, new campuses will have to be built. Within states, some institutions will lose students while others will grow. Some of the impact will depend upon responsiveness to the needs of nontraditional students and new groups of traditional-age students. For example, in some parts of our country, including the Midwest, a rapidly growing Hispanic population will desire postsecondary education.

Inflation and energy problems will have a differential impact. Residential institutions far from metropolitan areas will experience the changing conditions differently from large urban institutions accessible by mass transportation.

It is also my contention that the conventional assumption of a lowered sense of value or support for higher education will be greatly affected by the quality and vigor of leadership in our institutions and systems.

What I wish to do here is add some of my own assumptions about the environment in which we find ourselves that are more difficult to describe because we cannot quantify them. I want also to discuss the problem of identifying and encouraging appropriate leadership for the decade ahead. Finally, I want to describe what I see as the essential leadership needs for our colleges and universities in the decade ahead.

The Erosion of Leadership Authority

There is not much joy in being a college or university president today, partly because of the external constraints placed on presidents in addition to those resulting from problems of governance. Further, we in higher education have gradually eliminated considerable areas of presidential judgment and discretion by adopting uniform procedures, formulas, and policies that command our fealty more than does our good sense. As Ashworth (1978) has observed, "Like Pavlov's dogs, administrators bit by bit are being conditioned to stay within very limited and well-trodden paths by shocks, commands, intimidations, and orders" (p. 89).

One must add to this erosion of presidential autonomy the effects of a decade of anti-establishment fervor with its concomitant hostility toward our social institutions. Whatever else we may have been unsure of in the 1970s, we were arrogantly certain that the Establishment was corrupt and that those who led our institutions were a part of that illegitimate authority aimed at our oppression. "People are more important than institutions" was a slogan of the counterculture that struck a responsive chord even in aspiring middle-class youth. I am sure that many deans and presidents experienced, as I did, in the late 1960s the aggressive hostility that was rationalized thusly: "It's not personal, it's just that you are a symbol of the Establishment and its evil." (Frankly, I never did enjoy being a symbol.)

I will not venture into pop sociology here, but it is valid to bring into the discussion the loss of faith in our leaders and institutions resulting from the Vietnam war and Watergate and assassinations of an inspiring President and two great social leaders—Martin Luther King, Jr., and Robert Kennedy. The reader may wish to add other items to this lost leadership syndrome. I cite this syndrome here so we can understand the negative environment in which institutional leadership has existed. The pernicious events of our time were accompanied by a style of investigative journalism and media coverage that added to the suspicions held of anyone in positions of responsibility and authority.

John Gardner (1978), a keen observer and analyst of the problems of leadership, has written,

> The pervasive hostility of people toward all institutions and all symbols of authority today places a heavy burden on leadership. Moreover, there is something perverse in the modern temper that seeks to diminish or destroy exemplary figures. With compulsive thoroughness we search our heroes for the hidden flaw. A now-famous political figure once said to me, . . . "If the journalists encountered Adonis, they'd circle round and round him, find a pimple on his rear end, and write their stories about the pimple" (p. 134).

I believe, however, that the pendulum is swinging to a more positive view of the need for leadership and for the renewal of our social institutions. Americans can only be pessimistic for so long and then they want to get going and do something about it. This need to get on with life is certainly the case with youth for they long to be able to identify with life-affirming values and cannot sustain a diet of negativism too long. It seems to me, therefore, that as the decade of the 1970s ends, we are searching, in a variety of ways, for some means of rediscovering a sense of human value and purpose. I have no doubts, though, about the fragility of the reaching out. That is why I believe that sensitive and optimistic leadership is so necessary for the 1980s.

I have spoken of youth and the tendency toward optimism. The major concern I have about the internal environment of higher education in the decade ahead relates to our faculties—our teacher-scholars. There are two matters I wish to identify: that of faculty self-esteem and morale, and the danger of treating the faculty as scapegoats.

The Internal Environment
In the past decade, higher education experienced an attack on the liberal arts and on scientism. The authoritativeness of the curriculum was desanctified with attacks on its relevance and its Western rationalistic, technological bias. At first, the university was seen as a power base, to be captured and utilized for large-scale social change. Knowledge was power and the faculty possessed the knowledge to transform the nature of society if they wished. Through a relevant curriculum and courses devoted to peace, urban problems, and racism, we could alter the direction of our society. This view of academe was short-lived and followed by a repudiation of the significance of the university in the scheme of things. Faculty were often treated as impotent and irrelevant. Currently, there is a wave of enrollment shifts to professional and applied subjects. Rather than being concerned with a subject's relevance to a social revolution,

students first assess a subject's utility in the job market. That attitude, too, will change, in my opinion.

My point in this portrayal is that in many ways our faculties have suffered a lengthy period of demoralization that affects their sense of commitment, pride in their work, satisfaction with their career choice, and the like. Many of them were once applauded for possessing competence in areas or subjects now seen as arcane. It is difficult to celebrate the fact that you have committed your life to that of scholar-teacher, only to find that, rather than the intrinsic value of your devotion being sufficient, your worth is also being assessed by the declining number of student credit hours you are producing. Being good at something no one seems to value does not provide much satisfaction.

The lack of faculty mobility, the so-called Ph.D. glut, adds to this problem. Perceptive presidents have described to me, in poignant terms, the bitterness and hostility of some faculty, trapped in a teaching situation in an institution they never thought would be more than a stepping-stone in an illustrious career. Such persons, seeing no alternative other than to remain for the rest of their teaching careers in institutions they see as out of phase with their aspirations and talents, lash out at both administrators and students. Alienated from both their institutions and authority, they become the leaders of faculty councils and unions. Yet they are the key people to whom a new president must turn in seeking to renew an institution.

The other matter relating to the internal environment of higher education over the next ten years is the danger that faculty will be treated as scapegoats. I refer to the faculty, and particularly tenured faculty, being regarded as a *problem,* because they are not easily dismissed or interchanged with new, or younger, or different faculty. It is not unusual to hear tenure attacked, or senior faculty portrayed as "deadwood." The howls of some institution leaders when retirement age was advanced to age seventy was indicative of the message—we wish we did not have to keep you so long and if you would leave we could bring in more vital people (at less salary) to invigorate us. Often administrators and board members respond to criticism of their institution's inertia by blaming the faculty, claiming they are a group of reactionaries who, protected by tenure, resist any innovation or modernization. Obviously, there are individuals who fit such a description. Yet, on the whole, we add to the problem of reduced faculty mobility by oversimplifying it and resorting to the stereotyping of faculty as recalcitrant foes of renewal and improvement. What we need is a kind of leadership that intervenes in this vicious circle and begins to lift us out of our predicament. The leader who is primarily motivated by an avoidance of personal blame is not needed. Too many others are using that script.

There are many good reasons for the faculty to feel as they do about their institutions and their leaders. If we make them the culprits in troubled times, to whom can we turn for improving our condition? The faculty is the core of the higher education enterprise. Without them, there is no enterprise.

The emphasis in this essay is on the characteristics of the presidency, rather than on the organizational characteristics of colleges and universities. But we in higher education will have to reexamine our organizational needs, as well. The tendency may be to hunker down and defend our territory in a last ditch stand against all foes. Instead, our organizational structures must be made more flexible and responsiveness must be facilitated and adaptability enhanced. Good ideas and personal initiatives must be encouraged and not stifled by structure. In many ways, we have to create a fail-safe method for ensuring that countervailing voices will be heard. Maintaining such openness is the best insurance against both inertia and faddishness.

If my assumptions are correct about the turbulent state ahead of us, how do we develop leadership for the future and what kind of leadership is required?

We have no formal system for training leaders in higher education. In the public elementary and secondary schools, a system of licensing or certification qualifies school or district administrators. It is a controversial system, at best, and not one to be emulated for our diverse postsecondary enterprise. Nevertheless, finding qualified higher education leaders continues to be a problem. In colleges and universities, leaders tend to be identified by their peers. The dominant coalition on a particular campus will identify one of their number who not only shares their values but also articulates and defends such values effectively. Such persons may be adopted by mentors. Eventually, such persons become *sponsored* by the leadership of their institutions—nominated for leadership training experiences under the aegis of national organizations, such as the American Council on Education, or nominated for positions at other institutions seeking deans, vice-presidents, and presidents. It is rare for persons to be purposefully groomed for the top leadership in their own institution because leadership succession is so quixotic in our higher learning institutions.

The problem of identifying leadership is similar to that encountered in the search-and-screen process of presidential selection. Do any mavericks get through the screen or are the only ones who get through the conciliators whose definition of success may be survival?

John Gardner (1978), once again, comments on the obstacles to leadership and the problem of preserving a measure of creativity in the potential leader. He observes that,

All too often, on the long road up, young leaders become "servants of what is" rather than "shapers of what might be." In the long process of learning how the system works, they are rewarded for playing within the intricate structure of existing rules. By the time they reach the top, they are trained prisoners of the structure. This is not all bad: every vital system reaffirms itself. But ultimately no system can stay vital unless *some* of its leaders remain sufficiently independent to help it to change and grow (p. 135).

Will we have a problem in getting independent leaders to assume responsibility in our colleges and universities in a decade of turbulence or decline? Will those people who seek to make a difference through their efforts want more attractive opportunities in those sectors of our economy where there is the possiblity of expansion and greater creativity? Is it still possible for a college president to make much difference? Kenneth Boulding (1975) writes of the greater skill that is required in managing decline, as compared to growth, and he uses the railroads to illustrate the problem. While some industries, such as textiles, were able to adjust to changing times, "in contrast, the railroads adjusted very badly and exhibit the trauma of decline in almost classical form—regulation, rigidity, and loss of the best management personnel to expanding industries" (p. 9). (I also find it interesting that we are once again discovering the value of railroads and seeking their renewal.)

Views on Effective Leadership for Higher Education

What are the kinds of leadership that we require in our colleges and universities? I think we need politically effective leadership, visible leadership, and leadership that cherishes the essential value of our educational institutions and their potential for dignifying humankind and shaping its destiny. Only with such leadership can we release the creative energies within our institutions that are the solution to our problem.

We often use the word *political* to mean something pejorative, which is unfortunate, because politically effective leadership is necessary, particularly in public higher education. I once heard someone describe two different approaches to public relations: that which seeks to find out what people want and caters to that; and that which knows what it needs to do and persuades people to accept that. Similarly with the concept of politically effective leadership, there are those presidents who are perceptive and tune in to the prejudices of the public and their elected representatives, pandering to their transitory whims. Those presidents may be popular but I do not consider that political effectiveness. In my terms, a president should know what is needed in the way of public support and be effective in terms of the extent to which he or she can build support for those needs.

The low-profile president may have been of value during the past decade. I believe we need *visible* leadership now—leaders who will teach

the public. I speak of what James MacGregor Burns (1978) calls "transforming" leadership. Although he is speaking of political, rather than
educational, leaders, his view is even more germane to this discussion:

> Leaders can also shape and alter and elevate the motives and values and
> goals of followers through the vital *teaching* role of leadership. This is
> *transforming* leadership. The premise of this leadership is that, whatever
> the separate interests persons might hold, they are presently or
> potentially united in the pursuit of "higher" goals, the realization of
> which is tested by the achievement of significant change that represents
> the collective or pooled interests of leaders and followers (pp. 425–26).

Burns makes clear that transforming leadership involves more than the
leader, but the follower as well, and in the day-to-day pursuit of common
goals they are hard to separate one from the other.

> Much of what commonly passes as leadership—conspicuous position-
> taking without followers or follow-through, posturing on various public
> stages, manipulation without general purpose, authoritarianism—is no
> more leadership than the behavior of small boys marching in front of a
> parade, who continue to strut along Main Street after the procession has
> turned down a side street toward the fairgrounds. Also, many apparent
> leaders will be only partial leaders. They may tap followers' motives or
> power bases; or they may take value-laden positions; or they may
> sharpen conflict; or they may operate at the final policy-making or
> implementation stages; or they may do some or all of these. The test of
> their leadership function is their contribution to change, measured by
> purpose drawn from collective motives and values (p. 427).

There is, of course, a risk in being a visible leader and attempting to
be a transforming leader. But in the years ahead, higher education will be
sorely tested. If we believe that our institutions have value, we must
articulate that value and achieve adequate understanding and support.
We must find leaders who are dedicated enough to the purpose of higher
education that they will expend themselves, if necessary, for that purpose.

I do not believe that a period of less student enrollment will harm
higher education. Nor do I believe that financial austerity will destroy us.
In many ways, it would be healthy for us to be required to revisit and
redefine the essence of our enterprise. We have gone through three
decades of expansion; we have accommodated growth. We could use a
breathing period to examine our deficits in quality and sort out our
priorities. If necessary, we could get back to the basic purposes of the
university from which we are often distracted.

I do not demean the skills of management for they are crucial for
implementing great purposes. But in and of themselves, those skills will
not be enough for the turbulent period ahead. In the conflict over the
allocation of public resources to the various social needs of society, and
in the conflict over reduction and reallocation within our colleges and

universities, there will be considerable anguish. Political skill will be desirable, but the indispensible ingredient of leadership will be a sense of trust that the leader will do the *right* thing with what limited discretion remains. To instill that trust means leaders will have to show they understand and are committed to the values that people with the best motives can follow. Leaders will have to show they appreciate the essence of our colleges and universities and why they were created and supported and esteemed for so many generations. Leaders must not confuse service and training and practical relevance of some courses—as important as that might be—with the even more important concern for the cultivation of serious knowledge, a concern with beauty, truth, justice, and life itself.

I am speaking of leaders who understand and care deeply about what Edward Shils calls the "capital" of a university:

> . . . that capital is much more than its physical plant or its library; it is also more than the stock of knowlege and skills that its academic staff members bring to their tasks. It includes the zeal for discovery, the moral integrity, the powers of discriminating judgment, the awareness of important problems, and the possibilities for their solution that their members possess. These are qualities of individuals, but their stable persistence depends on the existence of an academic community, within departments and faculties in the university as a whole and in the academic community at large—within the boundaries of the country and internationally (pp. 196–97).

The president will have to take initiatives, the consequences of which are important. Mistakes are easily covered in times of growth. Covering mistakes will not be very easy in the future. To attempt visible and transforming leadership is not to attempt a feat of a daring-do. Neither should the qualities of such leadership be confused with those of personal charisma. The qualities of transforming leadership are those that restore in organizations or society a sense of meaning and purpose and release the powerful capacity humankind has for renewal.

Teachers, students, and educational institutions not only shape expectations about the future but also create the future by the manner and quality of their interaction. Many forces in society compete to shape that future. Some people would hope that education will have the least effect in determining that future. They see our task as one which steers or bends students to adapt and adjust to the "reality" of the impending forces of our technology and our economy. They see any other approach as impractical or inefficient. They see the measure of human worth as denoted by humankind's elasticity and adaptability rather than by our convictions and resistance to the dehumanization about us. There is some legitimacy to demands that we in higher education be consumer oriented, productivity conscious, and output oriented. Yet we know higher learning is more complicated than those demands imply.

In thinking of the future, the conception that humankind has of itself should not be what it is today, but what we think we can become. We have nearly lost the art and the will of trying to convey to our children and to one another what it is we dare to become, what it is we cherish, what inspires us, what we hold dear. I think we shall be called to account for what higher education ought to become.

George Bonham (1974), editor of *Change* Magazine, has pointed out that the "understandable obsession with basic survival has deprived much of the academic leadership of any remaining energies to deal with the larger problems of the last quarter of this century. . . . The result of all this," he states, "is not only a poverty of spirit, but a much-reduced involvement of some of the nation's best minds with our cultural and academic futures" (p. 9).

It is my belief that human freedom is inextricably tied to the purposes of higher education—that one of higher education's functions is to encourage and to celebrate the potential of the human spirit. What higher education is all about relates to the human condition itself. For the future, then, a priority is to start a resistance movement against all those forces that shrivel the human spirit. I think the great challenge to all of us is essentially one of ethics. How do we encourage and preserve a reverence for life? How do we help life achieve its highest destiny? How do we develop the altruistic behavior that one associates with such goals? Unless we can make some progress in this direction, we will not truly be valued by all those we have the potential to serve.

I believe higher education and colleges and universities to be important to our future. Though I do not equate presidents with the same importance, nevertheless I believe that effective, good presidents are crucial to our institutions. There are no material incentives to attract the kind of people ready to give the dedicated service I believe necessary. Rather, the attraction is a sense of service—a calling, if you will—that at its best has a spiritual dimension. For presidential service links one with important and serious matters that have concerned men and women for centuries and will continue to do so.

When we look to our institutions, we tend to personalize them through their presidents. If we wish to place the institutions on trial, it is usually the president's quality of leadership that is the object of our attention. If we wish to demand that something be done, it is to the president we speak.

It is a source of amazement, then, that we can get good people to aspire to the role of president. It is equally amazing that we vest control of such vital institutions in the hands of unpaid, part-time lay governing boards. The future of higher education depends on the dedicated people I have described stepping forward to serve, for a while, "at the pleasure of the board."

Epilogue

The Athenians had a custom of selecting a speaker to deliver a panegyric at the burial of those who fell in battle. Though the situation of college and university presidents may not be analogous to that of people who defended Athenian democracy, these presidents are men and women of valor whose efforts and worth I have tried to represent in this essay. As the Athenian panegyrist Pericles said when he began his oration with these words, so, too, do I:

> I could have wished that the reputations of many brave men were not to be imperiled in the mouth of a single individual, to stand or fall as he spoke well or ill. For it is hard to speak properly upon a subject where it is even difficult to convince your hearers that you are speaking the truth. On the one hand, the friend, who is familiar with every fact of the story, may think that some point has not been set forth with that fullness which he wishes and knows it to deserve; on the other hand, he who is a stranger to the matter may be led by envy to suspect exaggeration if he hears anything above his own nature. For men can endure to hear others praised only so long as they can severally persuade themselves of their own ability to equal the actions recounted: When this point is passed, envy comes in and with it incredulity.

References

American Association of State Colleges and Universities. "Guidelines for Conditions of Employment for College and University Presidents." Washington, D.C.: The Association, 1975.

American Association of University Professors. "1940 Statement of Principles on Academic Freedom and Tenure." In *AAUP Policy Documents and Reports,* 1977 ed. Washington, D.C.: The Association.

American Association of University Professors. "Statement on Government of Colleges and Universities" [1966]. In *AAUP Policy Documents and Reports,* 1977 ed. Washington, D.C.: The Association.

American Scholar. "In Memoriam—The College President." Editorial. Summer 1949, pp. 265–70.

Anderson, G. Lester. "The Evaluation of Academic Administrators." Paper delivered at a conference, "Running Higher Education," of the Council for the Advancement of Small Colleges and the American Association for Higher Education, Airlie House, Feburary 1–4, 1977.

Ashby, Eric. *Adapting Universities to a Technological Society.* San Francisco: Jossey-Bass, 1974.

Ashworth, Kenneth H. *American Higher Education in Decline.* College Station: Texas A&M Press, 1979.

Association of Governing Boards of Universities and Colleges. "Self-Study Guidelines and Criteria for Governing Boards." Washington, D.C.: The Association, 1976.

Baldridge, J. Victor. *Power and Conflict in the University.* New York: John Wiley & Sons, 1971.

Baldridge, J. Victor; Curtis, David V.; Ecker, George; and Riley, Gary L. *Policy Making and Effective Leadership.* San Francisco: Jossey-Bass, 1978.

Beadle, Muriel. *Where Has All the Ivy Gone?* Garden City, N.Y.: Doubleday, 1972.

Bennis, Warren. *The Unconscious Conspiracy.* New York: AMACOM, 1976.

Block, Murray H. "State University of New York: Presidential Evaluation." In *Administrator Evaluation,* ed. Charles H. Farmer. Richmond, Va.: Higher Education Leadership and Management Society, Inc., 1979.

Bonham, George. "Change and the Academic Future." *Change,* June 1974.

Boulding, Kenneth E. "The Management of Decline." *Change,* June 1975.

Bowen, Howard R. *Academic Compensation.* New York: Teachers Insurance & Annuity Association, 1978.

Burns, James MacGregor. *Leadership.* New York: Harper & Row, 1978.

"By-Laws of the Board of Regency University System of Illinois." Springfield, Ill.: 1972.

Carnegie Commission on Higher Education. *Governance of Higher Education: Six Priority Problems.* New York: McGraw-Hill, 1973.

Carnegie Commission on Higher Education. *Priorities for Action: Final Report of the Carnegie Commission on Higher Education.* New York: McGraw-Hill, 1973.

Cattell, James McKeen. *University Control.* New York: Science Press, 1913.

Cleveland, Harlan. "The Education of Administrators for Higher Education." Fourth David D. Henry Lecture, University of Illinois, 1977.

Cohen, Michael D., and March, James G. *Leadership and Ambiguity.* New York: McGraw-Hill, 1974.

Corbally, Marguerite Walker. *The Partners: Sharing the Life of a College President.* Danville, Ill.: Interstate, 1977.

Corson, John. *The Governance of Colleges and Universities.* New York: McGraw-Hill, 1960, revised 1975.

Cowley, W. H. "What Does a College President Do?" Address at the inauguration of Roy E. Lieuallen as president of Oregon College of Education, Feb. 5, 1956.

Daly, Lowrie J. *The Medieval University.* New York: Sheed & Ward, 1961.

Demerath, Nicholas J., et al. *Power, Presidents and Professors.* New York: Basic Books, 1967.

Dodds, Harold W. *The Academic President—Educator or Caretaker?* New York: McGraw-Hill, 1962.

Drucker, Peter. *The Effective Executive.* New York: Harper & Row, 1966.

Farmer, Charles H., ed. *Administrator Evaluation.* Richmond, Va.: Higher Education Leadership and Management Society, Inc., 1979.

Fisher, Charles F., ed. *Developing and Evaluating Administrative Leadership.* New Directions for Higher Education, no. 22. San Francisco: Jossey-Bass, 1978.

FTU Presidential Search Advisory Committee. "Final Report on the Selection of a New President, Florida Technological University." Submitted to the Board of Regents, Orlando, Florida, February 1978.

Gardner, John W. *Morale*. New York: W. W. Norton & Co., 1978.

Greenleaf, Robert K. *Servant Leadership*. New York: Paulist Press, 1977.

Greenleaf, Walter J. "New College Presidents." *School and Society*, Jan. 11, 1936, pp. 61–62.

Harper, William Rainey. "The College President." *Educational Record*, April 1938, pp. 178–86. (Prepared in 1904.)

Harvard University, University Committee on Governance. "Discussion Memorandum Concerning the Choice of a New President." Cambridge, Mass.: April 1970.

Henry, David D. *Challenges Past, Challenges Present*. San Francisco: Jossey-Bass, 1975.

Hutchins, Robert Maynard. *Freedom, Education and the Fund: Essays and Addresses, 1946–1956*. New York: Meridian Books, 1956.

Hyde, Robert M. "The Presidential Search: Chore or Opportunity?" *Educational Record*, Spring 1969, pp. 186–88.

"The Impossible Job?" In a Special Report. Washington, D.C.: Editorial Projects for Education, Inc., 1976.

Jencks, Christopher, and Riesman, David. *The American Revolution*. Garden City, N.Y.: Doubleday, 1968.

Kaplowitz, Richard A. "The Impact of Sunshine/Open Meeting Laws on the Governing Boards of Public Colleges and Universities." MS. Washington, D.C.: Association of Governing Boards of Universities and Colleges, July 1978.

Kauffman, Joseph F. "The New College President: Expectations and Realities." *Educational Record*, Spring 1977, pp. 146–68.

Kauffman, Joseph F. "Presidential Assessment and Development." In *Developing and Evaluating Administrative Leadership*, ed. Charles F. Fisher. New Directions for Higher Education, no. 22. San Francisco: Jossey-Bass, 1978.

Kauffman, Joseph F. *The Selection of College and University Presidents*. Washington, D.C.: Association of American Colleges, 1974.

Kauffman, Joseph F., and Walker, Donald E. "The College President: Expectations, Realities and Myths." Papers from the 17th Annual Meeting of the American Association of State Colleges and Universities, Washington, D.C., 1978.

Kemerer, Frank R., and Baldridge, J. Victor. *Unions on Campus*. San Francisco: Jossey-Bass, 1975.

Kerr, Clark. "Presidential Discontent." In *Perspectives on Campus Tensions*, ed. David C. Nichols. Washington, D.C.: American Council on Education, 1970.

Kerr, Clark. *The Uses of the University.* Cambridge, Mass.: Harvard University Press, 1963 and 1972.

Lee, Eugene C., and Bowen, Frank M. *The Multicampus University.* New York: McGraw-Hill, 1971.

Monson, Charles H., Jr. "Metaphors for the University." *Educational Record,* Winter 1967, pp. 22–29.

Munitz, Barry. "Reviewing Presidential Leadership." In *Handbook of College and University Trusteeship,* by Richard T. Ingram and Associates. San Francisco: Jossey-Bass, under the auspices of the Association of Governing Boards of Universities and Colleges, 1980.

Nason, John W. *The Future of Trusteeship: The Role and Responsibilities of College and University Boards.* Washington, D.C.: Association of Governing Boards of Universities and Colleges, 1974.

Nason, John. *Presidential Assessment: A Challenge to College and University Leadership.* Washington, D.C.: Association of Governing Boards of Universities and Colleges, 1980.

Nason, John W. *Presidential Search.* Washington, D.C.: Association of American Colleges, 1979.

National Center for Education Statistics, U.S. Department of Health, Education, and Welfare. *Education Directory: Colleges and Universities, 1976–1977* and *1978–79.* Washington: Government Printing Office.

New York State Regents' Advisory Committee on Educational Leadership. James A. Perkins et al. "College and University Presidents: Recommendations and Report of a Survey." 1967. (ED015552)

Perkins, James A., ed. *The University as an Organization.* New York: McGraw-Hill, 1973.

Redfern, Leo F. "Single Governing Boards in Multicampus Systems." MS, July 1979.

Sarason, Seymour B. *The Creation of Settings and the Future Societies.* San Francisco: Jossey-Bass, 1972.

Semas, Philip W. "The Perilous Presidencies." *Chronicle of Higher Education,* Feb. 3, 1975.

Shils, Edward. "Governments and Universities." In *The University and the State: What Role for Government in Higher Education?"* ed. Sidney Hook, Paul Kurtz, and Miro Todorovich. Buffalo, N.Y.: Prometheus Books, 1978.

Sinclair, Upton. *The Goose-Step: A Study of American Education.* Pasadena: John Regan & Co., 1923.

State University of New York, Board of Trustees. "Policies of the Board of Trustees." Albany, N.Y.: SUNY, 1977.

Stimson, Henry A. "The Evolution of the College President." *American Monthly Review of Reviews,* April 1899, pp. 451–53.

Stoke, Harold W. *The American College President.* New York: Harper & Brothers, 1959.

Tucker, Allan, and Mautz, Robert B. "Presidential Evaluation: An Academic Circus." *Educational Record,* Summer 1979, pp. 253–60.

Thwing, Charles F. *College Administration*. New York: Century, 1900.

U.S. Office of Education, Department of Health, Education, and Welfare. *The College Presidency, 1900–1960: An Annotated Bibliography,* by Walter Crosby Eells and Ernest V. Hollis. Washington, D.C.: Government Printing Office, 1961.

Veblen, Thorstein. *The Higher Learning in America*. Stanford, Calif.: Academic Reprints, 1954. P. 85.

Veysey, Laurence R. *The Emergence of the American University*. Chicago: University of Chicago Press, 1965.

Wells, Herman B. "Points of View." *Bulletin of the International Association of Universities,* August 1965.

Yarmolinsky, Adam. "Institutional Paralysis." *Daedalus,* Winter 1975.

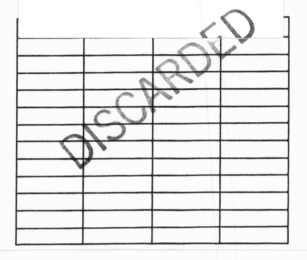